THE 22 IMMUTABLE LAWS OF MARKETING

Al Ries and Jack Trout run a marketing consulting firm in Greenwich, Connecticut, servicing clients from AT&T to Weyerhaeuser, and are the authors of the international bestsellers *Positioning, Marketing Warfare*, *Bottom-Up Marketing* and *Focus*.

Also by Al Ries

Focus

with Laura Ries

The 22 Immutable Laws of Branding

AL RIES AND JACK TROUT

The 22 Immutable Laws of Marketing

PROFILE BOOKS

Published in Great Britain by
PROFILE BOOKS LTD
3A Exmouth House
Pine Street
Exmouth Market
London EC1R 0JH
www.profilebooks.com

First published in Great Britain by
HarperCollins*Publishers* in 1994

9 10

Printed and bound by CPI Group (UK) Ltd, Croydon, CR0 4YY

A CIP catalogue record for this book is available from the British Library.

ISBN-10: 1 86197 610 0
ISBN-13: 978 1 86197 610 9

Dedicated to the elimination of myths and misconceptions from the marketing process

Contents

Introduction

Billions of dollars have been wasted on marketing programs that couldn't possibly work, no matter how clever or brilliant. Or how big the budgets.

Many managers assume that a well-designed, well-executed, well-financed marketing program will work. It's not necessarily so. And you don't have to look further than IBM, General Motors, and Sears, Roebuck to find examples.

The tools and techniques used at Sears, Roebuck might have been right, sometimes even spectacular. And the managers who ran the GM programs might have been the best and the brightest. Certainly the best and the brightest people traditionally have been attracted to the biggest and the best companies, like GM and IBM. But the programs themselves were based on assumptions that were flawed.

John Kenneth Galbraith, when asked what he believed was America's perception of the country's giant corporations, said that we feared corporate power. Today, we fear corporate incompetence!

INTRODUCTION

All companies are in trouble. Especially big companies. General Motors is a good example. Over the past decade the company paid a terrible price for destroying the identity of its brands. (It priced them alike as well as made them look alike.) Ten share points evaporated, which translates into about $10 billion a year in sales.

GM's problem wasn't a competitive problem, although competition did increase. It wasn't a quality problem either, although GM obviously wasn't delivering top-notch quality. It was very definitely a marketing problem.

When a company makes a mistake today, footprints quickly show up on its back as competition runs off with its business. To get the business back, the company has to wait for others to make mistakes and then figure out how to exploit the situation.

So how do you avoid making mistakes in the first place? The easy answer is to make sure your programs are in tune with the laws of marketing. (Although we have defined our ideas and concepts under the "marketing" banner, they are useful no matter where you are in a company, and no matter what product or service your company is selling.)

What are these marketing laws? And who brought them down from Mount Sinai on a set of stone tablets?

The fundamental laws of marketing are those described in this book.

But who says so? How come two guys from Connecticut have discovered what thousands of others have overlooked? There are, after all, many sophisticated marketing practitioners and academics. Why have they missed what we think is so obvious?

The answer is simple. As far as we can tell, almost no one is willing to admit that there are any laws of marketing—certainly none that are immutable.

There are laws of nature, so why shouldn't there be laws of marketing? You can build a great-looking airplane, but it's not going to get off the ground unless it adheres to the laws of physics, especially the law of gravity. You can build an architectural masterpiece on a sand dune, but the first hurricane will undermine your creation. So it follows that you can build a brilliant marketing program only to have one of the immutable laws knock you flat if you don't know what they are.

Perhaps it's human nature not to admit there are things you can't do. Certainly most marketers believe that anything is achievable if you are energetic enough, or creative enough, or determined enough. Especially if you are willing to spend enough money.

Once you open your mind to the possibility that there are laws of marketing, it's easy to see what they are. In truth, they are obvious.

We have been studying what works in marketing and what doesn't for more than 25 years. What we have found is that programs that work are almost always in tune with some fundamental force in the marketplace.

In our books, articles, speeches, and videos we have analyzed marketing principles in some detail. We have developed strategic models of the marketing process, including a physical model of the human mind, which we helped popularize under the concept of "positioning." We also developed a military model of the marketplace, which assigns companies and brands to either defensive, offensive, flanking, or guerrilla modes of marketing warfare.

After years of working on marketing principles and problems, we have distilled our findings into the basic laws that govern success and failure in the marketplace.

We call these principles the Immutable Laws of Marketing, and there are 22 of them. Violate them at your own risk.

The 22 Immutable Laws of Marketing

1
The Law of Leadership

It's better to be first than it is to be better.

Many people believe that the basic issue in marketing is convincing prospects that you have a better product or service.

Not true. If you have a small market share and you have to do battle with larger, better-financed competitors, then your marketing strategy was probably faulty in the first place. You violated the first law of marketing.

The basic issue in marketing is creating a category you can be first in. It's the law of leadership: It's better to be first than it is to be better. It's much easier to get into the mind first than to try to convince someone you have a better product than the one that did get there first.

You can demonstrate the law of leadership by asking yourself two questions:

1) What's the name of the first person to fly the Atlantic Ocean solo? Charles Lindbergh, right?
2) What's the name of the second person to fly the Atlantic Ocean solo? Not so easy to answer, is it?

The second person to fly the Atlantic Ocean solo was Bert Hinkler. Bert was a better pilot than Charlie—he flew faster, he consumed less fuel. Yet who has ever heard of Bert Hinkler? (He left home and Mrs. Hinkler hasn't heard from him since.)

In spite of the evident superiority of the Lindbergh approach, most companies go the Bert Hinkler route. They wait until a market develops. Then they jump in with a better product, often with their corporate name attached. In today's competitive environment, a me-too product with a line extension name has little hope of becoming a big, profitable brand (chapter 12: The Law of Line Extension).

The leading brand in any category is almost always the first brand into the prospect's mind. Hertz in rent-a-cars. IBM in computers. Coca-Cola in cola.

After World War II, Heineken was the first imported beer to make a name for itself in America. So four decades later, what is the No. 1 imported beer? The one that tastes the best? Or Heineken? There are 425 brands of imported beer sold in America. Surely one of these brands must taste better than Heineken, but does it really matter? Today, Heineken is still the No. 1 imported beer, with 30 percent of the market.

The first domestic light beer was Miller Lite. So what is the largest-selling light beer in America today? The one that tastes the best? Or the one that got into the mind first?

Not every first is going to become successful, however. Timing is an issue—your first could be too late. For example, *USA Today* is the first national newspaper, but it is unlikely to succeed. It has already lost $800 million and has never had a profitable year. In a television era, it may be too late for a national newspaper.

Some firsts are just bad ideas that will never go anywhere. Frosty Paws, the first ice cream for dogs, is unlikely to make it. The dogs love it, but the owners are the ones who buy the groceries, and they think that dogs don't need an ice cream of their own. They should be happy just to lick the plates.

The law of leadership applies to any product, any brand, any category. Let's say you didn't know the name of the first college founded in America. You can always make a good guess by substituting *leading* for *first*. So what's the name of the leading college in America? Most people would probably say Harvard, which is also the name of the first college founded in America. (What's the name of the second college founded in America? The College of William and Mary, which is only slightly more famous than Bert Hinkler.)

No two products are any similar than twins are. Yet twins often complain that the first of the two whom a person meets always remains their favorite, even though the person also gets to know the other one.

People tend to stick with what they've got. If you meet someone a little better than your wife or husband, it's really not worth making the switch, what with attorneys' fees and dividing up the house and kids.

The law of leadership also applies to magazines. Which is why *Time* leads *Newsweek*, *People* leads *Us*, and *Playboy* leads *Penthouse*. Take *TV Guide*, for example. Back in the early fifties the then-powerful Curtis Publishing Company tried to field a television-listings magazine to compete with the fledgling *TV Guide*. Even though *TV Guide* had only a minuscule head start, and despite the awesome strength of Curtis, the Curtis publication never really got off the ground. *TV Guide* had preempted the field.

The law of leadership applies equally as well to hard categories like automobiles and computers as it does to soft categories like colleges and beer. Jeep was first in four-wheel-drive off-the-road vehicles. Acura was first in luxury Japanese cars. IBM was first in mainframe computers. Sun Microsystems was first in workstations. Jeep, Acura, IBM, and Sun are all leading brands.

The first minivan was introduced by Chrysler. Today Chrysler has 10 percent of the car market and 50 percent of the minivan market. Is the essence of car marketing making better cars or getting into the market first?

The first desktop laser printer was introduced by a computer company, Hewlett-Packard. Today the company has 5 percent of the personal computer market and 45 percent of the laser printer market.

Gillette was the first safety razor. Tide was the first laundry detergent. Hayes was the first computer modem. Leaders all.

One reason the first brand tends to maintain its leadership is that the name often becomes generic. Xerox, the first plain-paper copier, became the name for all plain-paper copiers. People will stand in front of a Ricoh or a Sharp or a Kodak machine and say, "How do I make a Xerox copy?" They will ask for the Kleenex when the box clearly says Scott. They will offer you a Coke when all they have is Pepsi-Cola.

How many people ask for cellophane tape instead

of Scotch tape? Not many. Most people use brand names when they become generic: Band-Aid, Fiberglas, Formica, Gore-Tex, Jello, Krazy Glue, Q-tips, Saran Wrap, Velcro—to name a few. Some people will go to great lengths to turn a brand name into a generic. "FedEx this package to the Coast." If you're introducing the first brand in a new category, you should always try to select a name that can work generically. (Lawyers advise the opposite, but what do they know about the laws of marketing?)

Not only does the first brand usually become the leader, but also the sales order of follow-up brands often matches the order of their introductions. The best example is ibuprofen. Advil was first, Nuprin was second, Medipren was third. That's exactly the sales order they now enjoy: Advil has 51 percent of the ibuprofen market, Nuprin has 10 percent, and Medipren has 1 percent.

The fourth brand that entered the market was Motrin IB. Even though it has the powerful prescription name for ibuprofen, Motrin's market share is only 15 percent. (Keep in mind that Advil was introduced with a "Same as the prescription drug Motrin" theme.) And note the generic substitution. Consumers use *Advil* as a generic term. Rarely do they use the word *ibuprofen*. Even an M.D. will tell a patient, "Take two Advil and call me in the morning."

Also consider Tylenol, the first brand of acetaminophen. Tylenol is so far ahead of the No. 2 brand that it's hard to determine who *is* No. 2.

If the secret of success is getting into the prospect's mind first, what strategy are most companies committed to? The better-product strategy. The latest and hottest subject in the business management field is benchmarking. Touted as the "ultimate competitive strategy," benchmarking is the process of comparing and evaluating your company's products against the best in the industry. It's an essential element in a process often called "total quality management."

Unfortunately, benchmarking doesn't work. Regardless of reality, people perceive the first product into the mind as superior. Marketing is a battle of perceptions, not products.

So what's the name of the first brand of aspirin? The first brand of acetaminophen? The first brand of ibuprofen? (Hint: Substitute *leading* for *first* and you'll have the answers to these three questions.)

Charles Schwab bills itself as "America's largest discount broker." Are you surprised that the Charles Lindbergh of the discount brokerage business is Charles Schwab?

Neil Armstrong was the first person to walk on the moon. Who was second?

Roger Bannister was the first person to run a four-minute mile. Who was second?

George Washington was the first president of the United States. Who was second?

Thomas' was the first brand of English muffin. What was second?

Gatorade was the first sports drink. What was second?

If you're second into the prospect's mind, are you doomed to languish forever with Buzz Aldrin, John Landy, John Adams, some unknown English muffin, and some unknown sports drink? Not necessarily. Fortunately, there are other laws.

2
The Law of the Category

If you can't be first in a category, set up a new category you can be first in.

What's the name of the third person to fly the Atlantic Ocean solo?

If you didn't know that Bert Hinkler was the second person to fly the Atlantic, you might figure you had no chance at all to know the name of the third person. But you do. It's Amelia Earhart.

Now, is Amelia known as the third person to fly the Atlantic Ocean solo, or as the first woman to do so?

After Heineken became a big success, the people at Anheuser-Busch could have said, "We should bring in an imported beer, too." But they didn't. Instead they said, "If there's a market for a high-priced imported beer, maybe there's a market for a high-priced domestic beer." And so they started to promote Michelob, the first high-priced domestic beer, which today outsells Heineken two to one. (Actually, Anheuser-Busch also brought in an imported beer, Carlsberg, which has a very good reputation in Europe. In the United States, however, the me-too Carlsberg never went anywhere.)

Miller Lite was the first domestic light. It took an importer five years to say, "If there's a market for a domestic light beer, maybe there's a market for an imported light beer." The result was Amstel Light, which became the largest-selling imported light beer.

If you didn't get into the prospect's mind first, don't give up hope. Find a new category you can be first in. It's not as difficult as you might think.

After IBM became a big success in computers, everybody and his brother jumped into the field. Burroughs, Control Data, General Electric, Honeywell, NCR, RCA, Sperry. Snow White and the seven dwarfs, they were called.

Which dwarf grew up to become a worldwide powerhouse, with 126,000 employees and sales of $14 billion, a company often dubbed "the second largest computer company in the world"? None of them. The most successful computer company of the seventies and eighties, next to IBM, was Digital Equipment Corporation. IBM was first in computers. DEC was first in minicomputers.

Many other computer companies (and their entrepreneurial owners) became rich and famous by following a simple principle: If you can't be first in a category, set up a new category you can be first in.

Tandem was first in fault-tolerant computers and built a $1.9 billion business. So Stratus stepped down with the first fault-tolerant minicomputer. Today Stratus is a $500 million company.

Are the laws of marketing difficult? No, they are quite simple. Working things out in practice is another matter, however.

Cray Research went over the top with the first supercomputer. Today, Cray is an $800 million company. So Convex put two and two together and launched the first minisupercomputer. Today, Convex is a $200 million company.

Sometimes you can turn an also-ran into a winner by inventing a new category. Commodore was just another manufacturer of home personal computers that wasn't going anywhere until it positioned the

Amiga as the first multimedia computer. Today the Commodore Amiga is a big success, with more than $500 million worth sold annually.

There are many different ways to be first. Dell got into the crowded personal computer field by being the first to sell computers by phone. Today Dell is a $900 million company.

When you launch a new product, the first question to ask yourself is not "How is this new product better than the competition?" but "First what?" In other words, what category is this new product first in?

Charles Schwab didn't open a better brokerage firm. He opened the first discount broker.

Lear's was not the first woman's magazine. It was the first magazine for the mature woman. (The magazine for the woman who wasn't born yesterday.)

This is counter to classic marketing thinking, which is brand oriented: How do I get people to prefer my brand? Forget the brand. Think categories. Prospects are on the defensive when it comes to brands. Everyone talks about why their brand is better. But prospects have an open mind when it comes to categories. Everyone is interested in what's new. Few people are interested in what's better.

When you're the first in a new category, promote the category. In essence, you have no competition. DEC told its prospects why they ought to buy a minicomputer, not a DEC minicomputer.

In the early days, Hertz sold rent-a-car service. Coca-Cola sold refreshment. Marketing programs of both companies were more effective back then.

3
The Law of the Mind

It's better to be first in the mind than to be first in the marketplace.

INTRODUCED IN 1974

INTRODUCED IN 1976

The world's first personal computer was the MITS Altair 8800.

The law of leadership would suggest that the MITS Altair 8800 (an unfortunate choice of names) ought to be the No. 1 personal computer brand. Unfortunately, the product is no longer with us.

Du Mont invented the first commercial television set. Duryea introduced the first automobile. Hurley introduced the first washing machine. All are gone.

Is something wrong with the law of leadership in chapter 1? No, but the law of the mind modifies it. It's better to be first in the prospect's mind than first in the marketplace. Which, if anything, understates the importance of being first in the mind. Being first in the mind is everything in marketing. Being first in the marketplace is important only to the extent that it allows you to get in the mind first.

For example, IBM wasn't first in the marketplace with the mainframe computer. Remington Rand was first, with UNIVAC. But thanks to a massive marketing effort, IBM got into the mind first and won the computer battle early.

The law of the mind follows from the law of perception. If marketing is a battle of perception, not product, then the mind takes precedence over the marketplace.

Thousands of would-be entrepreneurs are tripped up every year by this law. Someone has an idea or concept he or she believes will revolutionize an industry, as well it may. The problem is getting the idea or concept into the prospect's mind.

The conventional solution to the problem is money. That is, the resources to design and build product or service organizations plus the resources to hold press conferences, attend trade shows, run advertisements, and conduct direct mail programs (chapter 22: The Law of Resources).

Unfortunately, this gives rise to the perception that the answer to all marketing questions is the same: money. Not true. More money is wasted in marketing than in any other human activity (outside of government activities, of course).

You can't change a mind once a mind is made up. It's like going head-to-head against an entrenched enemy, the charge of the Light Brigade at Balaclava being history's most famous example, closely followed by Pickett's fiasco at Gettysburg.

Wang was first in word processors. But the world passed such machines by and went on to computers. Wang, however, wasn't able to make the transition. In spite of spending millions of dollars promoting its personal computers and minicomputers, Wang is still perceived as a word processor company.

Xerox was first in copiers and then tried to get into the computer business. Twenty-five years and $2 billion later, Xerox is nowhere in computers.

You want to change something in a computer? Just type over or delete the existing material. You want to change something in a mind? Forget it. Once a mind is made up, it rarely, if ever, changes. The single most wasteful thing you can do in marketing is try to change a mind.

That accounts for the mystery of the well-formed opinion that can almost instantly appear in a person's mind. One day you've never heard of a person. The next day that person is famous. The "overnight sensation" is not an unusual phenomenon.

If you want to make a big impression on another person, you cannot worm your way into their mind and then slowly build up a favorable opinion over a period of time. The mind doesn't work that way. You have to blast your way into the mind.

The reason you blast instead of worm is that people don't like to change their minds. Once they perceive you one way, that's it. They kind of file you away in their minds as a certain kind of person. You cannot become a different person in their minds.

One of the mysteries of marketing is the role of money. One day a few dollars can work a major miracle. The next day millions of dollars can't save a company from going under. When you have an open mind to work with, even a small amount of money can go a long way. Apple got off the computer ground with $91,000 contributed by Mike Markkula.

Apple's problem in getting into its prospects' minds was helped by its simple, easy-to-remember name. On the other hand, Apple's competitors had complicated names that were difficult to remember. In the early days, five personal computers were in position on the launching pad: Apple II, Commodore Pet, IMSAI 8080, MITS Altair 8800, and Radio Shack TRS-80. Ask yourself, which name is the simplest and easiest to remember?

4
The Law of Perception

Marketing is not a battle of products, it's a battle of perceptions.

Many people think marketing is a battle of products. In the long run, they figure, the best product will win.

Marketing people are preoccupied with doing research and "getting the facts." They analyze the situation to make sure that truth is on their side. Then they sail confidently into the marketing arena, secure in the knowledge that they have the best product and that ultimately the best product will win.

It's an illusion. There is no objective reality. There are no facts. There are no best products. All that exists in the world of marketing are perceptions in the minds of the customer or prospect. The perception is the reality. Everything else is an illusion.

All truth is relative. Relative to your mind or the mind of another human being. When you say, "I'm right and the next person is wrong," all you're really saying is that you're a better perceiver than someone else.

Most people think they are better perceivers than others. They have a sense of personal infallibility. Their perceptions are always more accurate than those of their neighbors or friends. Truth and perception become fused in the mind, leaving no difference between the two.

It's not easy to see that this is so. To cope with the terrifying reality of being alone in the universe, people project themselves on the outside world. They "live" in the arena of books, movies, television, newspapers, magazines. They "belong" to clubs, organizations, institutions. These outside representations of the world seem more real than the reality inside their own minds.

People cling firmly to the belief that reality is the world outside of the mind and that the individual is one small speck on a global spaceship. Actually it's the opposite. The only reality you can be sure about is in your own perceptions. If the universe exists, it exists inside your own mind and the minds of others. That's the reality that marketing programs must deal with.

There may well be oceans, rivers, cities, towns, trees, and houses out there, but there just isn't any way for us to know these things except through our own perceptions. Marketing is a manipulation of those perceptions.

Most marketing mistakes stem from the assumption that you're fighting a product battle rooted in reality. All the laws in this book are derived from the exact opposite point of view.

What some marketing people see as the natural laws of marketing are based on a flawed premise that the product is the hero of the marketing program and that you'll win or lose based on the merits of the product. Which is why the natural, logical way to market a product is invariably wrong.

Only by studying how perceptions are formed in the mind and focusing your marketing programs on those perceptions can you overcome your basically incorrect marketing instincts.

Each of us (manufacturer, distributor, dealer, prospect, customer) looks at the world through a pair of eyes. If there is objective truth out there, how would we know it? Who would measure it? Who would tell us? It could only be another person looking at the same scene through a different pair of eye-windows.

Truth is nothing more or less than one expert's perception. And who is the expert? It's someone who is perceived to be an expert in the mind of somebody else.

If truth is so illusive, why is there so much discussion in marketing about the so-called facts? Why are so many marketing decisions based on factual comparisons? Why do so many marketing people assume that truth is on their side, that their job is to use truth as a weapon to correct the misperceptions that exist in the mind of the prospect?

Marketing people focus on facts because they believe in objective reality. It's also easy for marketing people to assume that truth is on their side. If you think you need the best product to win a marketing battle, then it's easy to believe you have the best product. All that's required is a minor modification of your own perceptions.

Changing a prospect's mind is another matter. Minds of customers or prospects are very difficult to change. With a modicum of experience in a product category, a consumer assumes that he or she is right. A perception that exists in the mind is often interpreted as a universal truth. People are seldom, if ever, wrong. At least in their own minds.

It's easier to see the power of perception over product when the products are separated by some distance. For example, the three largest-selling Japanese imported cars in America are Honda, Toyota, and Nissan. Most marketing people think the battle between the three brands is based on quality, styling, horsepower, and price. Not true. It's what people *think* about a Honda, a Toyota, or a Nissan that determines which brand will win. Marketing is a battle of perceptions.

Japanese automobile manufacturers sell the same cars in the United States as they do in Japan. If marketing were a battle of products, you would think the same sales order would hold true for both countries. After all, the same quality, the same styling, the same horsepower, and roughly the same prices hold true for Japan as they do for the United States. But in Japan, Honda is nowhere near the leader. There, Honda is in third place, behind Toyota and Nissan. Toyota sells more than four times as many automobiles in Japan as Honda does.

So what's the difference between Honda in Japan and Honda in the United States? The products are the same, but the perceptions in customers' minds are different.

If you told friends in New York you bought a Honda, they might ask you, "What kind of car did you get? a Civic? an Accord? a Prelude?" If you told friends in Tokyo you bought a Honda, they might ask you, "What kind of motorcycle did you buy?" In Japan, Honda got into customers' minds as a manufacturer of motorcycles, and apparently most people don't want to buy a car from a motorcycle company.

How about an opposite situation? Would Harley-Davidson be successful if it launched a Harley-Davidson automobile? You might think it would depend on the car. Quality, styling, horsepower, pricing. You might even believe the Harley-Davidson reputation for quality would be a plus. We think not. Its perception as a motorcycle company would undermine a Harley-Davidson car—no matter how good the product (chapter 12: The Law of Line Extension).

Why is Campbell's soup No. 1 in the United States and nowhere in the United Kingdom? Why is Heinz soup No. 1 in the United Kingdom and a failure in the United States? Marketing is a battle of perceptions, not products. Marketing is the process of dealing with those perceptions.

Some soft-drink executives believe that marketing is a battle of taste. Well, New Coke is No. 1 in taste. (The Coca-Cola Company conducted 200,000 taste tests that "proved" that New Coke tastes better than Pepsi-Cola and Pepsi tastes better than their original formula, now called Coca-Cola Classic.) But who is winning the marketing battle? The drink that research has proven to taste the best, New Coke, is in third place. The one that research shows tastes the worst, Coca-Cola Classic, is in first place.

You believe what you want to believe. You taste what you want to taste. Soft-drink marketing is a battle of perceptions, not a battle of taste.

What makes the battle even more difficult is that customers frequently make buying decisions based on second-hand perceptions. Instead of using their own perceptions, they base their buying decisions on someone else's perception of reality. This is the "everybody knows" principle.

Everybody knows that the Japanese make higher-quality cars than the Americans do. So people make buying decisions based on the fact that everybody knows the Japanese make higher-quality cars. When you ask shoppers whether they have had any personal experience with a product, most often they say they haven't. And, more often than not, their own experience is often twisted to conform to their perceptions.

If you have had a bad experience with a Japanese car, you've just been unlucky, because everybody knows the Japanese make high-quality cars. Conversely, if you have had a good experience with an American car, you've just been lucky, because everybody knows that American cars are poorly made.

Everybody knows there's a problem with Audi cars. On November 23, 1986, CBS broadcast a "60 Minutes" segment called "Out of Control." It called attention to a number of complaints about Audi's "unintended acceleration." American sales of Audis fell through the floorboards—from 60,000 in 1986 to 12,000 in 1991. But have you ever personally had any problems with "unintended acceleration" while test-driving an Audi? It is unlikely. Every single automobile expert who has tested the car has failed to duplicate the complaint. Yet the perception lingers on.

Recently Audi has been running advertisements comparing its cars to comparable cars made by Mercedes-Benz and BMW. According to the ads, German automotive experts rated Audi cars ahead of both Mercedes and BMW.

Do you believe that? Probably not. Is it true? Does it matter?

Marketing is not a battle of products. It's a battle of perceptions.

5
The Law of Focus

The most powerful concept in marketing is owning a word in the prospect's mind.

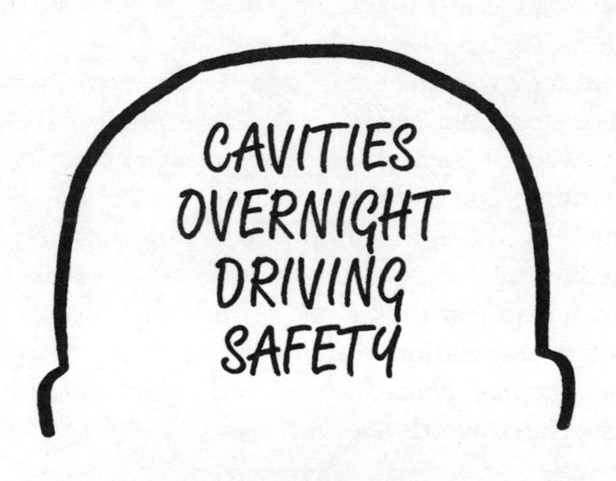

A company can become incredibly successful if it can find a way to own a word in the mind of the prospect. Not a complicated word. Not an invented one. The simple words are best, words taken right out of the dictionary.

This is the law of focus. You "burn" your way into the mind by narrowing the focus to a single word or concept. It's the ultimate marketing sacrifice.

Federal Express was able to put the word *overnight* into the minds of its prospects because it sacrificed its product line and focused on overnight package delivery only.

In a way, the law of leadership—it's better to be first than to be better—enables the first brand or company to own a word in the mind of the prospect. But the word the leader owns is so simple that it's invisible.

The leader owns the word that stands for the category. For example, IBM owns *computer.* This is another way of saying that the brand becomes a generic name for the category. "We need an IBM machine." Is there any doubt that a computer is being requested?

You can also test the validity of a leadership claim by a word association test. If the given words are *computer, copier, chocolate bar,* and *cola,* the four most associated words are *IBM, Xerox, Hershey's,* and *Coke.*

An astute leader will go one step further to solidify

its position. Heinz owns the word *ketchup*. But Heinz went on to isolate the most important ketchup attribute. "Slowest ketchup in the West" is how the company is preempting the thickness attribute. Owning the word *slow* helps Heinz maintain a 50 percent market share.

If you're not a leader, then your word has to have a narrow focus. Even more important, however, your word has to be "available" in your category. No one else can have a lock on it.

You don't have to be a linguistic genius to find a winner. Prego went against leader Ragu in the spaghetti sauce market and captured a 27 percent share with an idea borrowed from Heinz. Prego's word is *thicker*.

The most effective words are simple and benefit oriented. No matter how complicated the product, no matter how complicated the needs of the market, it's always better to focus on one word or benefit rather than two or three or four.

Also, there's the halo effect. If you strongly establish one benefit, the prospect is likely to give you a lot of other benefits, too. A "thicker" spaghetti sauce implies quality, nourishing ingredients, value, and so on. A "safer" car implies better design and engineering.

Whether the result of a deliberate program or not, most successful companies (or brands) are the ones that "own a word" in the mind of the prospect. (Some words, like Volkswagen's *fahrvergnugen*, are not worth owning.) Here are a few examples:

Crest. . . cavities
Mercedes. . . engineering
BMW. . . driving
Volvo. . . safety
Domino's. . . home delivery
Pepsi-Cola. . . youth
Nordstrom. . . service

Words come in different varieties. They can be benefit related (cavity prevention), service related (home delivery), audience related (younger people), or sales related (preferred brand).

Although we've been touting that words stick in the mind, nothing lasts forever. There comes a time when a company must change words. It's not an easy task. The recent history of Lotus Development Corporation demonstrates the nature of the problem.

For a number of years, Lotus has owned the word *spreadsheet*. *Lotus* was synonymous with *1-2-3* and *spreadsheet*. But the world of spreadsheets is getting competitive, and the potential for growth is limited. Like other companies, Lotus wants to grow. How is the company to get beyond its single-product business?

The conventional answer is to expand in all directions, as IBM and Microsoft did. As a matter of fact, Lotus did some conventional line extension with the purchase of Ami Pro word processing software and the introduction of a number of new software products. Then Lotus regrouped to focus on a new concept called "groupware," software products for networked PCs.

Lotus was the first software company to develop a successful groupware product. If things work out, the company will eventually own a second word in the minds of its prospects.

Unlike Microsoft, Lotus now has a corporate focus. It won't happen overnight, but Lotus could develop a powerful long-term position in the software field. What *overnight* did for Federal Express and *safety* did for Volvo, *groupware* could do for Lotus Development Corporation.

You can't take somebody else's word. What makes the Lotus strategy plausible is that the *groupware* word is not owned by any other company. Furthermore, there is an enormous industry trend toward networked computers. (More than half of all business computers are connected to a network. There's even a new magazine called *Network Computing.*) Many companies see the advantage of owning a single word or concept (often called "the corporate vision"), but they neglect to be the first to preempt the word.

What won't work in marketing is leaving your own word in search of a word owned by others. This was the case with Atari, which owned the words *video game*. But the business turned out to be faddish, so in 1982 it sailed off in a new direction. It wanted *Atari* to mean *computers.* CEO James Morgan laid it all out: "Atari's strength as a name also tends to be its weakness. It is synonymous with video games. Atari must redefine its image and broaden its business definition to electronic consumer products."

Unfortunately for Mr. Morgan's strategy, a host of

other companies, including Apple and IBM, owned the word he was after. Atari's diversification was a disaster. But the real irony was in that another company arrived in 1986 and took over the concept Atari walked away from. The company was Nintendo, which today has 75 percent of a multibillion-dollar market. Who knows where Atari is these days?

The essence of marketing is narrowing the focus. You become stronger when you reduce the scope of your operations. You can't stand for something if you chase after everything.

Some companies accept the need to narrow the focus and try to accomplish this strategy in ways that are self-defeating. "We'll focus on the quality end of the market. We won't get into the low end where the emphasis is on price." The problem is that customers don't believe you unless you restrict your business to high-priced products only, like Mercedes-Benz or BMW.

General Motors tries to sell quality at all price levels. "Putting quality on the road" is their latest corporate slogan. Every GM product includes the "Mark of Excellence." Guess what they're doing at Ford? The same thing. "Quality is Job 1," say the Ford ads. Over at Chrysler, Lee Iacocca proclaimed, "We don't want to be the biggest, we just want to be the best." (Does anyone really believe that Iacocca doesn't want to be the biggest?)

This is great stuff inside the corporation. Total quality, the path to greatness. It makes a terrific theme at dealer meetings, especially with the trumpet flourishes and the dancers. But outside the corporation, the message falls apart. Does any company proclaim itself as the "unquality" corporation? No, everybody stands for quality. As a result, nobody does.

You can't narrow the focus with quality or any other idea that doesn't have proponents for the opposite point of view. You can't position yourself as an honest politician, because nobody is willing to take the opposite position (although there are plenty of potential candidates). You can, however, position yourself as the pro-business candidate or the pro-labor candidate and be instantly accepted as such because there is support for the other side.

When you develop your word to focus on, be prepared to fend off the lawyers. They want to trademark everything you publish. The trick is to get others to use your word. (To be a leader you have to have followers.) It would be helpful for Lotus to have other companies get into the groupware business. It would make the category more important and people would be even more impressed with Lotus's leadership.

Once you have your word, you have to go out of your way to protect it in the marketplace. The case of BMW illustrates this very well. For years, BMW was the ultimate "driving" machine. Then the company decided to broaden its product line and chase Mercedes-Benz with large, 700-series sedans. The problem is, how can a living room on wheels be the ultimate driving machine? Not only can you not feel the road, but you'll also crush all the pylons in your driving commercials.

As a result, things started downhill for BMW. Luckily, it has recently introduced a new small BMW and is emphasizing "driving" once again. The company has regained its focus.

The law of focus applies to whatever you're selling, or even whatever you're unselling. Like drugs, for example. The antidrug crusade on television and in magazines suffers from a lack of focus. There is no one word driven into the minds of drug users that could begin to unsell the drug concept. Antidrug advertising is all over the map.

You'd think the antidrug forces (who, after all, are professionals) would have taken a leaf from the amateurs fighting the abortion issue. Both sides of the abortion issue have focused on single, powerful words—*pro-life* and *pro-choice.*

The antidrug forces should do the same—focus on a single powerful word. What the campaign ought to do is make drugs what cigarettes are today, socially unacceptable. One word that could do this is the ultimate down word, *loser.* Since drug usage causes all kinds of losses (of job, family, self-esteem, freedom, life), a program that said "Drugs are for losers" could have a very powerful impact, especially on the recreational user, who is more concerned with social status than with getting high.

The law of focus, a marketing law, could help solve one of society's biggest problems.

6
The Law of Exclusivity

Two companies cannot own the same word in the prospect's mind.

When a competitor owns a word or position in the prospect's mind, it is futile to attempt to own the same word.

As we mentioned earlier, Volvo owns *safety*. Many other automobile companies, including Mercedes-Benz and General Motors, have tried to run marketing campaigns based on safety. Yet no one except Volvo has succeeded in getting into the prospect's mind with a safety message.

The Atari story shows the futility of attempting to move in on the home computer position against well-entrenched competitors. A variation called *game computer* might have been possible because it would have taken advantage of the perception of Atari as a creator of computer games. But that's about it. The home computer position belonged to Apple, Commodore, and others.

Despite the disaster stories, many companies continue to violate the law of exclusivity. You can't change people's minds once they are made up. In fact, what you often do is reinforce your competitor's position by making its concept more important.

Federal Express has walked away from *overnight* and is in the middle of trying to take *worldwide* away from DHL. "Overnight Letter" used to be emblazoned on Federal Express envelopes. Today you'll find "FedEx Letter" instead. And its advertising no longer says, "When it absolutely, positively has to be there overnight." Lately the word that has been appearing in Federal Express advertising is *worldwide*.

This raises the all-important question: Can Federal Express ever own the *worldwide* word? Probably not. Someone else already owns it: DHL Worldwide Express. Its concept: Faster to more of the world. To succeed, Federal Express must find a way to narrow the focus against DHL. The company can't do it by trying to own the same word in the prospect's mind.

Another massive marketing effort aimed at someone else's word can be found in bunny land—to be specific, the pink Energizer bunny that is trying to take the "long-lasting" concept away from Duracell. No matter how many bunnies Eveready throws into the fray, Duracell will still be able to hang onto the *long-lasting* word. Duracell got into the mind first and preempted the concept. Even the *Dura* part of the name communicates it.

What often leads marketers down this booby-trapped lane is that wonderful stuff called research. Armies of researchers are employed, focus groups conducted, questionnaires tabulated—and what comes back in a three-pound report is a wish list of attributes that users want from a product or service. So if that's what people want, that's what we should give them.

What's the biggest problem people have with batteries? They go dead at the most inconvenient times. So what's the No. 1 battery attribute? Long-lasting, of course. If long-lasting is what people want, that's what we should advertise. Right? Wrong.

What researchers never tell you is that some other company already owns the idea. They would rather encourage clients to mount massive marketing programs. The theory is that if you spend enough money, you can own the idea. Right? Wrong.

Some years ago Burger King started down this slippery slope from which it has never quite recovered. A market study showed that the most popular attribute for fast food was "fast" (no big surprise there). So Burger King did what most red-blooded marketers do. It turned to its advertising agency and said, "If the world wants fast, our advertising should tell them we're fast."

What was overlooked in the research was that McDonald's was already perceived as being the fastest hamburger chain in the country. *Fast* belonged to McDonald's. Undaunted by this, Burger King launched its campaign with the slogan "Best food for fast times." The program quickly became a disaster very nearly on a par with the one that involved "Herb." The advertising agency was fired, management was fired, the company was sold, and downward momentum was maintained.

Many people have paid the price for violating the law of exclusivity.

7
The Law of the Ladder

The strategy to use depends on which rung you occupy on the ladder.

While being first into the prospect's mind ought to be your primary marketing objective, the battle isn't lost if you fail in this endeavor. There are strategies to use for No. 2 and No. 3 brands.

All products are not created equal. There's a hierarchy in the mind that prospects use in making decisions.

For each category, there is a product ladder in the mind. On each rung is a brand name. Take the car rental category. Hertz got into the mind first and wound up on the top rung. Avis got in second and National got in third.

Your marketing strategy should depend on how soon you got into the mind and consequently which rung of the ladder you occupy. The higher the better, of course.

Take Avis, for example. For years the company advertised the high quality of its rent-a-car service. "Finest in rent-a-cars" was one of its campaigns. The reader looked at the ad and wondered, How could they have the finest rent-a-car service when they're not on the top rung of my ladder?

Then Avis did the one thing you have to do to make progress inside the mind of the prospect. They acknowledged their position on the ladder. "Avis is only No. 2 in rent-a-cars. So why go with us? We try harder."

For 13 years in a row, Avis had lost money. Then, when it admitted to being No. 2, it started to make money, lots of money. Shortly thereafter, the company was sold to ITT, which promptly ordered up the advertising theme, "Avis is going to be No. 1."

No, they're not, said the prospect. They're not on the top rung of my ladder. And to make the point, many picked up the phone and called Hertz. The campaign was a disaster.

Many marketing people have misread the Avis story. They assume the company was successful because it tried harder (i.e., it had the better service). But that wasn't it at all. Avis was successful because it related itself to the position of Hertz in the mind. (If trying harder were the secret of success, Harold Stassen would have been president many times over.)

Many marketers make the same mistake as Avis did. Currently, Adelphi University in Garden City, Long Island, is comparing itself (favorably) with Harvard. Wait a minute, says the high school senior, Adelphi is not on my college ladder. As you might expect, Adelphi is not very successful in attracting the top students.

The mind is selective. Prospects use their ladders in deciding which information to accept and which information to reject. In general, a mind accepts only new data that is consistent with its product ladder in that category. Everything else is ignored.

When Chrysler compared its cars with Honda, very few people traded in their Preludes and Accords for Plymouths and Dodges. The headline of one Chrysler ad said: "Comparing a *used* Dodge Spirit to a *new* Honda Accord seemed a little ridiculous. Until we saw the results." According to the ad, 100 people were asked to compare a Dodge Spirit with 70,000 miles on it to a new Honda Accord. The majority (58 out of 100) chose the used Dodge.

Ridiculous. (But not necessarily untrue.)

What about your product's ladder in the prospect's mind? How many rungs are there on your ladder? It depends on whether your product is a high-interest or a low-interest product. Products you use every day (cigarettes, cola, beer, toothpaste, cereal) tend to be high-interest products with many rungs on their ladders. Products that are purchased infrequently (furniture, lawn mowers, luggage) usually have few rungs on their ladders.

Products that involve a great deal of personal pride (automobiles, watches, cameras) are also high-interest products with many rungs on their ladders even though they are purchased infrequently.

Products that are purchased infrequently and involve an unpleasant experience usually have very few rungs on their ladders. Automobile batteries, tires, and life insurance are three examples.

The ultimate product that involves the least amount of pleasure and is purchased once in a lifetime has no rungs on its ladder. Ever hear of Batesville caskets? Probably not, although the brand has almost 50 percent of the market.

There's a relationship between market share and your position on the ladder in the prospect's mind. You tend to have twice the market share of the brand below you and half the market share of the brand above you.

For example, Acura was the first Japanese luxury car. Lexus was second. Infiniti was third. In a recent year, Acura sold 143,708 cars in the United States, Lexus sold 71,206 cars, and Infiniti sold 34,890. The relationship among the three brands is almost a mathematically correct 4-2-1. (The Acura-Lexus-Infiniti battle is in its early stages, where the cars are new and there's a lot of interest among the public and the press. In the long run, when the products are no longer exciting, another phenomenon occurs. See the next chapter: The Law of Duality.)

Marketing people often talk about the "three leading brands" in a category as if it were a battle of equals. It almost never is. The leader inevitably dominates the No. 2 brand and the No. 2 brand inevitably smothers No. 3. In baby food, it's Gerber, Beech-Nut, and Heinz. In beer, it's Budweiser, Miller, and Coors. In long-distance telephone service it's AT&T, MCI, and Sprint.

What's the maximum number of rungs on a ladder? There seems to be a rule of seven in the prospect's mind. Ask someone to name all the brands he or she remembers in a given category. Rarely will anyone name more than seven. And that's for a high-interest category.

According to Harvard psychologist Dr. George A. Miller, the average human mind cannot deal with more than seven units at a time. Which is why seven is a popular number for lists that have to be remembered. Seven-digit phone numbers, the seven wonders of the world, seven-card stud, Snow White and the seven dwarfs, the seven danger signals of cancer.

Sometimes your own ladder, or category, is too small. It might be better to be a small fish in a big pond than to be a big fish in a small pond. In other words, it's sometimes better to be No. 3 on a big ladder than No. 1 on a small ladder.

The top rung of the lemon-lime soda ladder was occupied by 7-Up. (Sprite was on the second rung.) In the soft-drink field, however, the cola ladder is much bigger than the lemon-lime ladder. (Almost two out of three soft drinks consumed in America are cola drinks.) So 7-Up climbed on the cola ladder with a marketing campaign called "The Uncola."

As tea is to coffee, 7-Up became the alternative to a cola drink. And 7-Up sales climbed to where the brand was the third largest-selling soft drink in America.

Unfortunately, in recent years 7-Up lost its grip on third place by violating one of the laws yet to be discussed (chapter 12: The Law of Line Extension).

The ladder is a simple, but powerful, analogy that can help you deal with the critical issues in marketing. Before starting any marketing program, ask yourself the following questions: Where are we on the ladder in the prospect's mind? On the top rung? On the second rung? Or maybe we're not on the ladder at all.

Then make sure your program deals realistically with your position on the ladder. More on how to do this later.

8
The Law of Duality

In the long run, every market becomes a two-horse race.

Early on, a new category is a ladder of many rungs. Gradually, the ladder becomes a two-rung affair.

In batteries, it's Eveready and Duracell. In photographic film, it's Kodak and Fuji. In rent-a-cars, it's Hertz and Avis. In mouthwash, it's Listerine and Scope. In hamburgers, it's McDonald's and Burger King. In sneakers, it's Nike and Reebok. In toothpaste, it's Crest and Colgate.

When you take the long view of marketing, you find the battle usually winds up as a titanic struggle between two major players—usually the old reliable brand and the upstart.

Back in 1969, there were three major brands of a certain product. The leader had about 60 percent of the market, the No. 2 brand had a 25 percent share, and the No. 3 brand had a 6 percent share. The rest of the market included either private label or minor brands. The law of duality suggests that these market shares are unstable. Furthermore, the law predicts that the leader will lose market share and No. 2 will gain.

Twenty-two years later, the leader dropped down to 45 percent of the market. The No. 2 brand has 40 percent, and No. 3 has 3 percent. The products are Coca-Cola, Pepsi-Cola, and Royal Crown cola, respectively, but the principles apply to brands everywhere.

Look at the three long-distance telephone companies. AT&T has 65 percent of the market, MCI has 17 percent, and Sprint has 10 percent. Who will win and who will lose in the telephone wars? While the future is unknowable (chapter 17: The Law of Unpredictability), a betting person would put his or her money on MCI. MCI has won the battle with Sprint for second place, so now MCI ought to become the upstart alternative to old, reliable AT&T.

Sprint is probably feeling very comfortable on the third rung of the ladder. Nine percent doesn't sound like much, but it translates to $6 billion in annual sales. And the market has been growing rapidly.

For the long term, however, Sprint is in serious trouble. Look what happened to Royal Crown cola. Back in 1969, the Royal Crown company revitalized its franchise system, 350 bottlers strong, and hired the former president of Rival Pet Foods and a veteran of both Coke and Pepsi. The company also retained Wells, Rich, Greene, a high-powered New York advertising agency. "We're out to kill Coke and Pepsi," declared Mary Wells Lawrence, the agency's head, to the Royal Crown bottlers. "I hope you'll excuse the word, but we're really out for the jugular."

The only brand that got killed was Royal Crown. In a maturing industry, third place is a difficult position to be in.

Take the domestic automobile industry. In spite of heroic measures undertaken by Lee Iacocca, Chrysler is in trouble. In the long run, marketing is a two-car race.

Take video games. In the late eighties, the market was dominated by Nintendo with a 75 percent share. The two also-rans were Sega and NEC. Today Nintendo and Sega are neck and neck, and NEC is way behind. In the long run, marketing is a two-game race.

Time frames, however, can vary. The fast-moving video game market played itself out in two or three seasons. The long-distance telephone market might take two or three decades.

Take the airline industry. American Airlines, with 20 percent of the market, got its nose out in front and will probably wind up as the Coca-Cola of the skies. The interesting battle is between Delta and United, tied at 18 percent apiece. One of these two will take off like Pepsi—the other is headed down with Royal Crown. In the long run, marketing is a two-airline race.

Are these results preordained? Of course not. There are other laws of marketing that can also affect the results. Furthermore, your marketing programs can strongly influence your sales, provided they are in tune with the laws of marketing. When you're a weak No. 3, like Royal Crown, you aren't going to make much progress by going out and attacking the two strong leaders. What they could have done is carved out a profitable niche for themselves (chapter 5: The Law of Focus).

Knowing that marketing is a two-horse race in the long run can help you plan strategy in the short run.

It often happens that there is no clearcut No. 2. What happens next depends upon how skillful the contenders are. Take the laptop computer field. Toshiba is in first place with 21 percent of the market. But there are five companies in second place.

Zenith, Compaq, NEC, Tandy, and Sharp each have between 8 and 10 percent of the market. It ought to be fun to watch six horses come around a turn where there's room for only two. Toshiba and who? Which one will finish second?

What's especially tragic from the economy's point of view are the resources wasted in many high-visibility categories like laptop computers. Currently there are 130 laptop brands on the market. The law of duality will see to it that very few of these brands will be around in the twenty-first century.

Look at the history of the automobile in the United States. In 1904, 195 different cars were assembled by 60 companies. Within the following 10 years, 531 companies were formed and 346 perished. By 1923, only 108 car makers remained. This number dropped to 44 by 1927. Today, Ford and General Motors dominate the domestic industry, with Chrysler's future in doubt.

Successful marketers concentrate on the top two rungs. Jack Welch, the legendary chairman and CEO of General Electric, said recently: "Only businesses that are No. 1 or No. 2 in their markets could win in the increasingly competitive global arena. Those that could not were fixed, closed, or sold." It's this kind of thinking that built companies like Procter & Gamble into the powerhouses they are. In 32 of its 44 product categories in the United States, P&G commands the No. 1 or No. 2 brands.

Early on, in a developing market, the No. 3 or No. 4 positions look attractive. Sales are increasing. New, relatively unsophisticated customers are coming into the market. These customers don't always know which brands are the leaders, so they pick ones that look interesting or attractive. Quite often, these turn out to be the No. 3 or No. 4 brands.

As time goes on, however, these customers get educated. They want the leading brand, based on the naive assumption that the leading brand must be better.

We repeat: The customer believes that marketing is a battle of products. It's this kind of thinking that keeps the two brands on top: "They must be the best, they're the leaders."

9
The Law of the Opposite

If you're shooting for second place, your strategy is determined by the leader.

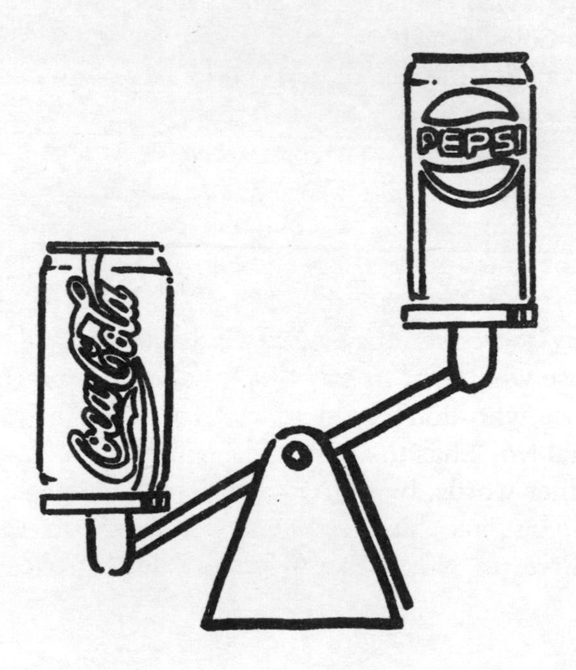

In strength there is weakness. Wherever the leader is strong, there is an opportunity for a would-be No. 2 to turn the tables.

Much like a wrestler uses his opponent's strength against him, a company should leverage the leader's strength into a weakness.

If you want to establish a firm foothold on the second rung of the ladder, study the firm above you. Where is it strong? And how do you turn that strength into a weakness?

You must discover the essence of the leader and then present the prospect with the opposite. (In other words, don't try to be better, try to be different.) It's often the upstart versus old reliable.

Coca-Cola is a 100-year-old product. Only seven people in the history of the world have known the Coke formula, which is kept locked in a safe in Atlanta. Coca-Cola is the old, established product. However, using the law of the opposite, Pepsi-Cola reversed the essence of Coca-Cola to become the choice of a new generation: the Pepsi Generation.

When you look at customers in a given product category, there seem to be two kinds of people. There are those who want to buy from the leader and there are those who don't want to buy from the leader. A potential No. 2 has to appeal to the latter group.

In other words, by positioning yourself against the leader, you take business away from all the other alternatives to No. 1. If old people drink Coke and young people drink Pepsi, there's nobody left to drink Royal Crown cola.

Yet, too many potential No. 2 brands try to emulate the leader. This usually is an error. You must present yourself as the alternative.

Time built its reputation on colorful writing. So *Newsweek* turned the idea around and focused on a straightforward writing style: "We separate facts from opinions." In other words, *Newsweek* puts its opinions in the editorial columns, not in the news columns.

Sometimes you need to be brutal. Scope, the good-tasting mouthwash, hung the "medicine breath" label on its Listerine competition.

But don't simply knock the competition. The law of the opposite is a two-edge sword. It requires honing in on a weakness that your prospect will quickly acknowledge. (One whiff of Listerine and you know that your mouth would smell like a hospital.) Then quickly twist the sword. (Scope is the good-tasting mouthwash that kills germs.)

Also in the mouthwash field is an interesting example of the futility of trying to emulate the leader. In 1961, Johnson & Johnson introduced Micrin mouthwash, focusing on its "scientific" virtues. Within months Micrin became the No. 2 brand. But with its germ-fighting approach, Listerine was also a scientific brand. So in 1965, when Procter & Gamble introduced Scope, it had the "opposite" position to itself. Scope went on to become the No. 2 mouthwash. By 1978, when Johnson & Johnson withdrew the product from the market, Micrin's share had fallen to 1 percent.

When Beck's beer arrived in the United States, it had a problem. It couldn't be the first imported beer (that was Heineken), nor could it be the first German imported beer (that was Lowenbrau). It solved its problem by repositioning Lowenbrau. "You've tasted the German beer that's the most popular in America. Now taste the German beer that's the most popular in Germany."

Today Beck's is the second largest-selling European beer in America. (When it comes to beer, Americans trust German mouths more than they do their own mouths.) This is a rare example of overturning the law of leadership and manipulating perceptions in the mind. (All this is academic today, since Lowenbrau is now brewed in America.)

As a product gets old, it often accrues some negative baggage. This is especially true in the medical field. Take aspirin, a product introduced in 1899. With thousands of medical studies conducted on aspirin, someone was bound to find flaws in the product. Sure enough, they found stomach bleeding—just in time for the 1955 launch of Tylenol.

With all the "stomach bleeding" publicity, Tylenol quickly was able to set itself up as the alternative. "For the millions who should not take aspirin," said the Tylenol advertising. Today Tylenol outsells aspirin and is the largest-selling single product in American drugstores.

Stolichnaya was able to hang the label of "fake

Russian vodka" on American vodkas such as Smirnoff, Samovar, and Wolfschmidt by simply pointing out that they come from places like Hartford (Connecticut), Schenley (Pennsylvania), and Lawrenceburg (Indiana). Stolichnaya comes from Leningrad (Russia), making it the real thing.

There has to be a ring of truth about the negative if it is to be effective. One of the classic examples of hanging a negative on a competitor is an advertisement that Royal Doulton China ran about its main U.S. competitor. The headline said it all: "Royal Doulton, the china of Stoke-on-Trent, England vs. Lenox, the china of Pomona, New Jersey." The ad exploited the fact that many people thought Lenox was an imported china. By repositioning Lenox where it really belonged, in Pomona, New Jersey, Royal Doulton was able to establish itself as the "real English china." Reason: Most people have a hard time imagining craftsmen making fine white-bone china in a tacky-sounding place like Pomona, New Jersey. (When the folks in England saw the ad, they howled with laughter. It turns out that Stoke-on-Trent is just as tacky as Pomona.)

Marketing is often a battle for legitimacy. The first brand that captures the concept is often able to portray its competitors as illegitimate pretenders.

A good No. 2 can't afford to be timid. When you give up focusing on No. 1, you make yourself vulnerable not only to the leader but to the rest of the pack. Take the sad story of Burger King in recent years. Times have been difficult for this No. 2 in hamburgers. It has been through many management changes, new owners, and a parade of advertising agencies. It doesn't take much of a history review to see what went wrong.

Burger King's most successful years came when it was on the attack. It opened with "Have it your way," which twitted McDonald's mass-manufacturing approach to hamburgers. Then it hit McDonald's with "Broiling, not frying" and "The Whopper beats the big Mac." All these programs reinforced the No. 2, alternative position.

Then, for some unknown reason, Burger King ignored the law of the opposite. It got timid and stopped attacking McDonald's. The world was introduced to "Herb the nerd," "The best food for fast times," "We do it the way you do it," "You've got to break the rules," and on and on. It even started a program to attract little kids, the mainstay of McDonald's strength.

This is no way to stay a strong No. 2. Burger King's sales per unit declined and have never returned to the level they were when it was on the attack.

Burger King made the mistake of not taking the opposite tack.

10
The Law of Division

Over time, a category will divide and become two or more categories.

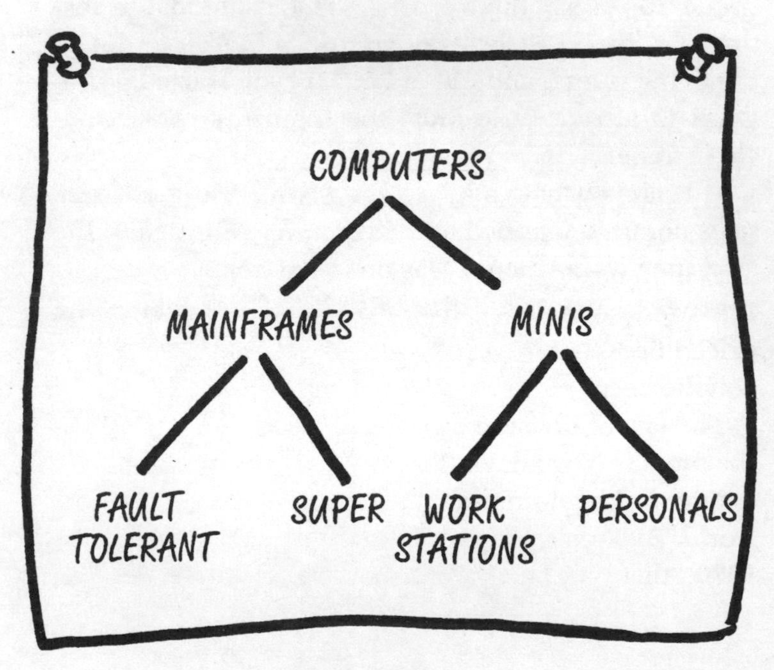

Like an amoeba dividing in a petri dish, the marketing arena can be viewed as an ever-expanding sea of categories.

A category starts off as a single entity. Computers, for example. But over time, the category breaks up into other segments. Mainframes, minicomputers, workstations, personal computers, laptops, notebooks, pen computers.

Like the computer, the automobile started off as a single category. Three brands (Chevrolet, Ford, and Plymouth) dominated the market. Then the category divided. Today we have luxury cars, moderately priced cars, and inexpensive cars. Full-size, intermediates, and compacts. Sports cars, four-wheel-drive vehicles, RVs, and minivans.

In the television industry, ABC, CBS, and NBC once accounted for 90 percent of the viewing audience. Now we have network, independent, cable, pay, and public television, and soon we'll have instore and interactive television.

Beer started the same way. Today we have imported and domestic beer. Premium and popular-priced beers. Light, draft, and dry beers. Even nonalcoholic beer.

The law of division even affects countries. (Witness the mess in Yugoslavia.) In 1776, there were about 35 empires, kingdoms, countries, and states in the world. By World War II, the number had doubled. By 1970, there were more than 130 countries. Today, some 190 countries are generally recognized as sovereign nations.

Look at the music field. It used to be classical and popular music. To stay on top of the popular music field you could watch "Your Hit Parade," which featured the top 10 hits of the week. Radio adopted the same idea with a "Top 40" format. Today Top 40 is falling apart because there isn't one list anymore.

Billboard, the bible of the music business, has 11 separate hit lists: classical, contemporary jazz, country, crossover, dance, Latin, jazz, pop, rap, rhythm and blues, and rock. And 11 leaders for the 11 categories. They recently included Itzhak Perlman, Fourplay, Garth Brooks, Luciano Pavarotti, Michael Jackson, Mi Mayor Necesidad, Dave Grusin, Enya, Public Enemy, Vanessa Williams, and Bruce Springsteen.

Each segment is a separate, distinct entity. Each segment has its own reason for existence. And each segment has its own leader, which is rarely the same as the leader of the original category. IBM is the leader in mainframes, DEC in minis, Sun in workstations, and so on.

Instead of understanding this concept of division, many corporate leaders hold the naive belief that categories are combining. *Synergy* and its kissing cousin the *corporate alliance* are the buzzwords in the boardrooms of America. IBM, according to the *New York Times*, is poised "to take advantage of the coming convergence of whole industries, including television, music, publishing and computing."

"IBM's strongest suit," says the *Times*, "in the

expected convergence of cable and telephone networks with computer and television manufacturers may be technology that it has developed to create extremely high-speed networks." (See chapter 20: The Law of Hype.)

It won't happen. Categories are dividing, not combining.

Also look at the much-touted category called "financial services." In the future, according to the press, we won't have banks, insurance companies, stockbrokers, or mortgage lenders. We'll have financial services companies. It hasn't happened yet.

Prudential, American Express, and others have fallen into the financial services trap. Customers don't buy financial services. They buy stocks or life insurance or bank accounts. And they prefer to buy each service from a different company.

The way for the leader to maintain its dominance is to address each emerging category with a different brand name, as General Motors did in the early days with Chevrolet, Pontiac, Oldsmobile, Buick, and Cadillac (and recently with Geo and Saturn).

Companies make a mistake when they try to take a well-known brand name in one category and use the same brand name in another category. A classic example is the fate that befell Volkswagen, the company that introduced the small-car category to America. Its Beetle was a big winner that grabbed 67 percent of the imported-car market in the United States.

Volkswagen was so successful that it began to think it could be like General Motors and sell bigger, faster, and sportier cars. So it swept up whatever models it was making in Germany and shipped them all to the United States. But unlike GM, it used the same brand, Volkswagen, for all of its models.

"Different Volks for different folks," said the advertising, which featured five different models, including the Beetle, the 412 Sedan, the Dasher, the Thing, and even a station wagon. Needless to say, the only thing that kept selling was the "small" thing, the Beetle.

Well, Volkswagen found a way to fix that. It stopped selling the Beetle in the United States and started selling a new family of big, fast, expensive Volkswagens. Now you had the Vanagon, the Sirocco, the Jetta, the Golf GL, and the Cabriolet. It even built a plant in Pennsylvania to build these wondrous new cars.

Unfortunately for Volkswagen, the small-car category continued to expand. And since people couldn't buy a long-lasting, economical VW, they shifted to Toyota, Honda, and Nissan.

Today Volkswagen's 67 percent share has shrunk to less than 4 percent.

Volkswagen isn't some minor European brand like Saab or Alfa Romeo. Volkswagen is the largest-selling automotive brand in Europe. The cars VW sells in the United States are the same as the ones it sells in Europe. Only the minds of the people buying them are different. In America, Volkswagen means small and ugly. Nobody here wants to buy a big, beautiful Volkswagen (chapter 4: The Law of Perception).

One of Volkswagen's competitors, Honda, decided to go up-market. Rather than use the Honda name in the luxury-car market, it introduced the Acura. It even took the expensive step of setting up separate Acura dealerships to avoid confusion with Honda.

The Acura became the first Japanese luxury car in the United States, where today Honda sells many more Acuras than Volkswagen sells Volkswagens. Honda now has the leading brand in two categories.

What keeps leaders from launching a different brand to cover a new category is the fear of what will happen to their existing brands. General Motors was slow to react to the superpremium category that Mercedes-Benz and BMW established. One reason was that a new brand on top of Cadillac would enrage GM's Cadillac dealers.

Eventually, GM tried to take Cadillac up-market with the $54,000 Allante. It bombed. Why would anyone spend that kind of money on a so-called Cadillac, since their neighbors would probably think they paid only $30,000 or so? No prestige.

A better strategy for General Motors might have been to put a new brand into the Mercedes market. (They might have brought back the classic LaSalle.)

Timing is also important. You can be too early to exploit a new category. Back in the fifties the Nash Rambler was America's first small car. But American Motors didn't have either the courage or the money to hang in there long enough for the category to develop.

It's better to be early than late. You can't get into the prospect's mind first unless you're prepared to spend some time waiting for things to develop.

11
The Law of Perspective

Marketing effects take place over an extended period of time.

Is alcohol a stimulant or a depressant?

If you visit almost any bar and grill on a Friday night after work, you'd swear that alcohol was a stimulant. The noise and laughter are strong evidence of alcohol's stimulating effects. Yet at 4:00 in the morning, when you see a few happy-hour customers sleeping it off in the streets, you'd swear that alcohol is a depressant.

Chemically, alcohol is a strong depressant. But in the short term, by depressing a person's inhibitions, alcohol acts like a stimulant.

Many marketing moves exhibit the same phenomenon. The long-term effects are often the exact opposite of the short-term effects.

Does a sale increase a company's business or decrease it? Obviously, in the short term, a sale increases business. But there's more and more evidence to show that sales decrease business in the long term by educating customers not to buy at "regular" prices.

Aside from the fact that you can buy something for less, what does a sale say to a prospect? It says that your regular prices are too high. After the sale is over, customers tend to avoid a store with a "sale" reputation.

To maintain volume, retail outlets find they have to run almost continuous sales. It's not unusual to walk down a retail block and find a dozen stores in a row with "Sale" signs in their windows.

Have the automobile rebate programs increased

sales? The rise of auto rebates have coincided with a decline in auto sales. U.S. vehicle sales have declined for five straight years in a row.

The largest furniture company in the New York City area, Seamans, has been running a sale every week. Recently, Seamans went bankrupt.

There is no evidence that couponing increases sales in the long run. Many companies find they need a quarterly dose of couponing to keep sales on an even keel. Once they stop couponing, sales drop off.

In other words, you keep those coupons rolling out not to increase sales but to keep sales from falling off if you stop. Couponing is a drug. You continue to do it because the withdrawal symptoms are just too painful.

Any sort of couponing, discounts, or sales tends to educate consumers to buy only when they can get a deal. What if a company never started couponing in the first place? In the retail field the big winners are the companies that practice "everyday low prices"—companies like Wal-Mart and K Mart and the rapidly growing warehouse outlets.

Yet almost everywhere you look you see yo-yo pricing. The airlines and the supermarkets are two examples. Recently, however, Procter & Gamble made a bold move to establish uniform pricing, which could become the start of a trend.

In everyday life there are many examples of short-term gains and long-term losses, crime being a typical example. If you rob a bank for $100,000 and wind up spending 10 years in jail, you either made

$100,000 for a day's work or $10,000 a year for 10 years of labor. It depends on your point of view.

Inflation can give an economy a short-term jolt, but in the long run, inflation leads to recession. (The nuts in Brazil haven't figured this out yet.)

In the short term, overeating satisfies the psyche, but in the long run it causes obesity and depression.

In many other areas of life (spending money, taking drugs, having sex) the long-term effects of your actions are often the opposite of the short-term effects. Why then is it so hard to comprehend that marketing effects take place over an extended period of time?

Take line extension. In the short term, line extension invariably increases sales. The beer industry clearly illustrates this effect. In the early seventies, Miller High Life was barreling along with sales increases averaging 27 percent a year. Miller's success was fueled by "Miller Time," a blue-collar campaign focused on rewarding yourself at the end of the day with a Miller beer. Then Miller got greedy and in 1974 introduced Miller Lite, a brilliant concept (chapter 2: The Law of the Category) buried under a line extended name.

In the short term the two Millers could coexist: the blue-collar beer (High Life) and the yuppie beer (Lite). But in the long term, line extension was bound to undermine one or the other brand.

The high-water mark for Miller High Life was 1979, five years after the introduction of Miller Lite. In those five years Miller High Life's annual sales almost tripled, from 8.6 million to 23.6 million barrels. This was the short-term effect of line extension.

The long-term effect was grim. From a high of 23.6 million barrels in 1979, Miller High Life declined 13 years in a row to just 5.8 million barrels in 1991. And the decline is bound to continue.

Nor has Miller Lite been immune to the ravages of line extension. In 1986, the brewer introduced Miller Genuine Draft. The brand took because it was the first beer in a new category. Unfortunately, the brand also carried the Miller name. (See the next chapter: The Law of Line Extension.) History repeats itself. Five years later, Miller Lite peaked in sales and then started to decline. Once started, the decline is almost impossible to stop.

Unless you know what to look for, it's hard to see the effects of line extension, especially for managers focused on their next quarterly report. (If a bullet took five years to reach a target, very few criminals would be convicted of homicide.)

The same thing that happened to Miller happened to Michelob. Three years after the introduction of Michelob Light, regular Michelob peaked in sales and then declined 11 years in a row. Today the four Michelob flavors combined (regular, light, dry, and classic dark) sell 25 percent fewer barrels than Michelob alone did in 1978, the year Michelob Light was introduced.

The same thing happened to Coors. The introduction of Coors Light caused the collapse of Coors regular, which today sells one-fourth of what it used to.

Even the king is down. After annual sales increases stretching back to the end of Prohibition, Budweiser has been slipping the last three years in a row. The cause? Bud Light.

You might be thinking that Miller, Coors, and Anheuser-Busch had to line extend because light beer has taken over the market. If you believe what you read in the papers, you'd think that everyone is drinking light beer. Not true. Today, 18 years after the introduction of Miller Lite, light beer still accounts for only 31 percent of the beer market.

In other areas of marketing, the short-term/long-term line extension effects occur much more rapidly. Coca-Cola clothes were introduced by Murjani in 1985. Two years later wholesale volume reached $250 million. The following year, the line dried up virtually overnight, saddling Murjani with millions of dollars' worth of inventory.

What happened to Coca-Cola clothes also happened to Donald Trump. At first, The Donald was successful. Then he branched out and put his name on anything the banks would lend him money for. What's a Trump? A hotel, three casinos, two condominiums, one airline, one shopping center.

Fortune magazine called Trump "an investor with a keen eye for cash flow and asset values, a smart marketer, a cunning wheeler-dealer." *Time* and *Newsweek* put The Donald on their covers.

Today Trump is $1.4 billion in debt. What made him successful in the short term is exactly what caused him to fail in the long term. Line extension.

It looks easy, but marketing is not a game for amateurs.

12
The Law of Line Extension

There's an irresistible pressure to extend the equity of the brand.

If violating any of our laws was a punishable offense, a large portion of corporate America would be in jail.

By far the most violated law in our book is the law of line extension. What's even more diabolical is that line extension is a process that takes place continuously, with almost no conscious effort on the part of the corporation. It's like a closet or a desk drawer that fills up with almost no effort on your part.

One day a company is tightly focused on a single product that is highly profitable. The next day the same company is spread thin over many products and is losing money.

Take IBM. Years ago when IBM was focused on mainframe computers, the company made a ton of money. Today IBM is into everything and barely breaking even. In 1991, for example, IBM's revenues were $65 billion. Yet the company wound up losing $2.8 billion. That's almost $8 million a day.

In addition to selling mainframe computers, IBM markets personal computers, pen computers, workstations, midrange computers, software, networks, telephones, you name it. IBM even tried to get into the home computer market with the PCjr.

Along the way, IBM dropped millions on copiers (sold to Kodak), Rolm (sold to Siemens), Satellite Business Systems (shut down), the Prodigy network (limping along), SAA, TopView, OfficeVision, and OS/2.

When a company becomes incredibly successful, it invariably plants the seeds for its future problems.

Take Microsoft, the most successful company in the software field. (Even though the company is one-fiftieth the size of General Motors, Microsoft's stock is worth more than GM's.) What is Microsoft's strategy? In a word, more.

"Microsoft Corp. said it is aggressively seeking the dominant share in every major software applications category in the personal computer field," said the *Wall Street Journal* recently. "Michael Maples, senior vice president of Microsoft's applications division, suggested that Microsoft might be able to achieve as much as a 70 percent share in every major applications category," continued the *Journal*.

Whom does that sound like? Sounds like IBM. Microsoft is setting itself up as the next IBM, with all the negative implications the name suggests.

Microsoft is the leader in personal computer operating systems, but it trails the leaders in each of the following major categories: spreadsheets (Lotus is the leader), word processing (WordPerfect is the leader), and business graphics (Harvard Graphics from SPC Software Publishing is the leader).

Microsoft keeps puffing itself up by expanding into new categories, such as pen computers. Recently, Microsoft bought Fox Software for $170 million in order to get into the data base software field. (What do you bet the company kills the *Fox* and changes it to *Microsoft?*)

There are ominous signs of softness in Microsoft's strategy. The *Economist* reported in early 1992, "Mr. Gates is putting together a range of products, based on a common core of technology, that will compete across virtually the whole of the software industry: from big computers to small ones, and from operating systems in the information engine-room to graphics programs that draw every picture for executives. Nobody in the software industry has yet managed a venture of that complexity—though IBM has tried and failed."

When you try to be all things to all people, you inevitably wind up in trouble. "I'd rather be strong somewhere," said one manager, "than weak everywhere."

In a narrow sense, line extension involves taking the brand name of a successful product (e.g., A-1 steak sauce) and putting it on a new product you plan to introduce (e.g., A-1 poultry sauce).

It sounds so logical. "We make A-1, a great sauce that gets the dominant share of the steak business. But people are switching from beef to chicken, so let's introduce a poultry product. And what better name to use than A-1. That way people will know the poultry sauce comes from the makers of that great steak sauce, A-1."

But marketing is a battle of perception, not product. In the mind, A-1 is not the brand name, but the steak sauce itself. "Would you pass me the A-1?" asks the diner. Nobody replies: "A-1 what?"

In spite of an $18 million advertising budget, the A-1 poultry launch was a dismal failure.

There are as many ways to line extend as there are galaxies in the universe. And new ways get invented every day. In the long run and in the presence of serious competition, line extensions almost never work.

Creating flavors is a popular way to try to grab market share. More flavors, more share. Sounds right, but it doesn't work.

Back in 1978, when 7-Up was simply the lemon-lime uncola, it had a 5.7 percent share of the soft-drink market. Then the company added 7-Up Gold, Cherry 7-Up, and assorted diet versions. Today 7-Up's share is down to 2.5 percent.

Wherever you look, you'll find line extensions, which is one reason why stores are choked with brands. (There are 1,300 shampoos, 200 cereals, 250 soft drinks.)

Invariably, the leader in any category is the brand that is not line extended. Take baby food, for example. Gerber has 72 percent of the market, way ahead of Beech-Nut and Heinz, the two line-extended brands.

In spite of evidence that line extensions don't work, companies continue to pump them out. Here are some examples:

Ivory soap. Ivory shampoo?
Life Savers candy. Life Savers gum?
Bic lighters. Bic pantyhose?
Chanel. Chanel for men?
Tanqueray gin. Tanqueray vodka?
Coors beer. Coors water?
Heinz ketchup. Heinz baby food?
USA Today. "USA Today on TV"?

Adidas running shoes. Adidas cologne?
Pierre Cardin clothing. Pierre Cardin wine?
Levi's blue jeans. Levi's shoes?

Colgate-Palmolive: "We want to leverage our basic core brands and trade on our brand names to extend into new categories." Ed Fogarty, President.

Campbell Soup Company: "Leveraging and extending high-quality, repeat-purchase brand names is always preferred over launching a new name." David W. Johnson, CEO.

Del Monte: "We're dedicated to the single brand concept. We're going to keep extending the Del Monte name into new areas." Ewan MacDonald, President.

Ultra Slim-Fast: "There will be soups, pastas, salad dressings, soda, fruit juices and a new, thicker diet drink called Ultra Slim-Fast Plus." Daniel Abraham, Chairman.

(Good luck and good night, Mr. Abraham.)

Why does top management believe that line extension works, in spite of the overwhelming evidence to the contrary? One reason is that while line extension is a loser in the long term, it can be a winner in the short term (chapter 11: The Law of Perspective). Management is also blinded by an intense loyalty to the company or brand. Why else would PepsiCo have introduced Crystal Pepsi in spite of the failures of Pepsi Light and Pepsi AM?

More is less. The more products, the more markets, the more alliances a company makes, the less money it makes. "Full-speed ahead in all directions" seems to be the call from the corporate bridge. When will companies learn that line extension ultimately leads to oblivion?

Less is more. If you want to be successful today, you have to narrow the focus in order to build a position in the prospect's mind.

What does IBM stand for? It used to stand for "mainframe computers." Today it stands for everything, which means it stands for nothing.

Why is Sears, Roebuck in trouble? Because the company tried to be all things to all people. Sears was big in hard goods, so it went into soft goods and then fashion. The company even hired Cheryl Tiegs. (Do fashion models really buy their miniskirts at Sears?)

In the conventional view, a business strategy usually consists of developing an all-encompassing vision. In other words, what concept or idea is big enough to hold all of a company's products and services on the market today as well as those that are planned for the future?

In the conventional view, strategy is a tent. You stake out a tent big enough so it can hold everything you might possibly want to get into.

IBM has erected an enormous computer tent. Nothing in the computer field, today or in the future, will fall outside the IBM tent. This is a recipe for disaster. As new companies, new products, new ideas invade the computer arena, IBM is going to get blown away. You can't defend a rapidly growing market like computers even if you are a financial powerhouse like IBM. From a strategic point of view, you have to be much more selective, picking and choosing the area in which to pitch your tent.

Strategically, General Motors is in the same boat as IBM. GM is into anything and everything on wheels. Sedans, sports cars, cheap cars, expensive cars, trucks, minivans, even electric cars. So what is GM's business strategy? If it runs on the road, or off the road, we'll chase it.

For many companies, line extension is the easy way out. Launching a new brand requires not only money, but also an idea or concept. For a new brand to succeed, it ought to be first in a new category (chapter 1: The Law of Leadership). Or the new brand ought to be positioned as an alternative to the leader (chapter 9: The Law of the Opposite). Companies that wait until a new market has developed often find these two leadership positions already preempted. So they fall back on the old reliable line extension approach.

The antidote for line extension is corporate courage, a commodity in short supply.

13
The Law of Sacrifice

You have to give up something in order to get something.

The law of sacrifice is the opposite of the law of line extension. If you want to be successful today, you should give something up.

There are three things to sacrifice: product line, target market, and constant change.

First, the product line. Where is it written that the more you have to sell, the more you sell?

The full line is a luxury for a loser. If you want to be successful, you have to reduce your product line, not expand it. Take Emery Air Freight. Emery was in the air freight services business. Anything you wanted to ship you could ship via Emery. Small packages, large packages, overnight service, delayed service.

From a marketing point of view, what did Federal Express do? It concentrated on one service: small packages overnight. Today Federal Express is a much bigger company than Emery.

The power of the sacrifice for Federal Express was in being able to put the word *overnight* in the mind of the prospect. When it absolutely, positively had to be there overnight, you would call Federal Express.

Then what did Federal Express do? The company did the same thing Emery did. It threw away its overnight position by buying Tiger International's Flying Tiger cargo line for $880 million. Now Federal Express is a worldwide air cargo company without a worldwide position. In just 21 months Federal Express lost $1.1 billion in its international operations.

Marketing is a game of mental warfare. It's a battle of perceptions, not products or services. In the mind of the prospect, Federal Express is the overnight company. Federal Express owns the overnight position. When the market turned international, Federal Express faced a classic marketing dilemma. Should it try to take a domestic name into the international field? Or should it create a new worldwide name? Furthermore, how should it deal with DHL, the company that got into the international field first?

It's bad enough that Federal Express walked away from the "overnight" idea. What's worse is that it didn't replace the idea with a new one.

Eveready was the long-time leader in batteries. But new technology arrived—as it does in most industries. The first technology to change the battery business was the heavy-duty battery. What would you call your heavy-duty battery if you had the No. 1 name in batteries? You'd probably call it the Eveready heavy-duty battery, which is what Eveready did.

Then the alkaline battery arrived. Again, Eveready called its alkaline battery the Eveready alkaline battery. It seemed to make sense.

Then P.R. Mallory introduced a line of alkaline batteries only. Furthermore, the company gave the line a better name: Duracell.

The power of the sacrifice for Duracell was in being able to put the "long-lasting battery" idea in the mind of the prospect. Duracell lasts twice as long as Eveready, said the advertising.

Eveready was forced to change the name of its

alkaline battery to "the Energizer." But it was too late. Duracell had already become the leader in the battery market.

The world of business is populated by big, highly diversified generalists and small, narrowly focused specialists. If line extension and diversification were effective marketing strategies, you'd expect to see the generalists riding high. But they're not. Most of them are in trouble.

The generalist is weak. Take Kraft, for example. Everybody thinks Kraft is a strong brand name. In jellies and jams, Kraft has 9 percent of the market. But Smucker's has 35 percent. *Kraft* means *everything,* but with a name like Smucker's, it has to be jelly or jam because that's all Smucker's makes. In mayonnaise, Kraft has 18 percent of the market. But Hellmann's has 42 percent.

(Kraft does have a leading brand in terms of market share. However, its name isn't *Kraft,* it's *Philadelphia*. Philadelphia brand cream cheese has 70 percent of the cream cheese market.)

Take the retail industry. Which retailers are in trouble today? The department stores. And what's a department store? A place that sells everything. That's a recipe for disaster.

Campeau, L.J. Hooker, and Gimbels all wound up in bankruptcy court. Ames department stores filed for bankruptcy. Hills department stores filed for bankruptcy. Macy's, the owner of the world's largest store, filed for bankruptcy.

Interstate Department Stores also went bankrupt.

So the company looked at the books and decided to focus on the only product it made money on: toys. As long as Interstate was going to focus on toys, it decided to change its name to Toys "Я" Us. Today Toys "Я" Us does 20 percent of the retail toy business in the country. Very profitably, too. In its last fiscal year, Toys "Я" Us made $326 million on sales of $5.5 billion.

Many retail chains are successfully patterning themselves on the Toys "Я" Us formula: a narrow focus with in-depth stock. Staples (office supplies) and Blockbuster Video are two recent examples.

In the retail field generally, the big successes are the specialists:

- The Limited. Upscale clothing for working women.
- The Gap. Casual clothing for the young at heart.
- Benetton. Wool and cotton clothing for young swingers.
- Victoria's Secret. Sexy undergarments.
- Foot Locker. Athletic shoes.
- Banana Republic. Safari wear.

(When a clothing chain with a name like Banana Republic can be successful, you know we live in the age of the specialist.)

Let's discuss the second sacrifice, target market. Where is it written that you have to appeal to everybody?

Take the cola field. Coca-Cola got into the prospect's mind first and built a powerful position. In the late fifties, for example, Coke outsold Pepsi more than five to one. What could Pepsi-Cola do to go against Coke's powerful position?

In the early sixties Pepsi-Cola finally developed a strategy based on the concept of sacrifice. The company sacrificed everything except the teenage market. Then it brilliantly exploited this market by hiring its icons: Michael Jackson, Lionel Richie, Don Johnson.

Within one generation, Pepsi closed the gap. Today it is only 10 percent behind Coca-Cola in total U.S. cola sales. (In the supermarket, Pepsi-Cola actually outsells Coca-Cola.)

In spite of Pepsi-Cola's success, however, the pressure for enlarging the tent is always present. Recently it succumbed to temptation. According to *Advertising Age*, "Pepsi-Cola Co. has outgrown the Pepsi generation. In a major marketing shift, flagship Pepsi will be pitched as the soft drink for the masses."

"Gotta have it" is Pepsi's new theme. The advertising shows older people like Yogi Berra and Regis Philbin drinking Pepsi.

"The one drawback of Pepsi advertising in the past has been a little too much focus on youth," says Phil Dusenberry of Pepsi's ad agency BBDO. "We could have made greater gains had we expanded our horizons to cast a wider net and catch more people."

According to *Fortune* magazine, Coca-Cola is the world's most powerful trademark. When an also-ran like Pepsi-Cola develops a narrowly focused strategy that puts it within an eyelash of the leader, why would it change its powerful strategy?

Why indeed! There seems to be an almost religious belief that the wider net catches more customers, in spite of many examples to the contrary.

Take Budweiser, for example. "When we go out to develop a plan for Budweiser, we have to cover everybody above 21 years of age, whether they're male, female, black, white, " says August Busch IV.

Look at cigarette advertisements, especially old cigarette ads. They invariably show both a man and a woman. Why? In an age when most smokers were men, cigarette manufacturers wanted to broaden their market. We got the men, let's go out and get the women, too.

So what did Philip Morris do? It narrowed the focus to men only. And then it narrowed the focus even more to a man's man, the cowboy. The brand was called Marlboro. Today, Marlboro is the largest-selling cigarette in the world. In the United States, Marlboro is the largest-selling cigarette among men *and* women.

The target is not the market. That is, the apparent target of your marketing is not the same as the people who will actually buy your product. Even though Pepsi-Cola's target was the teenager, the market was everybody. The 50-year-old guy who wants to think he's 29 will drink the Pepsi.

The target of Marlboro advertising is the cowboy, but the market is everybody. Do you know how many cowboys are left in America? Very few. (They've all been smoking Marlboros.)

Finally, the third sacrifice: constant change. Where

is it written that you have to change your strategy every year at budget review time?

If you try to follow the twists and turns of the market, you are bound to wind up off the road. The best way to maintain a consistent position is not to change it in the first place.

People Express had a brilliant "narrow" position to start with. It was the no-frills airline that flew to no-frills cities at no-frills prices. People used to get on a People Express plane and say, "Where are we going?" They didn't care, as long as it was cheap enough.

What did People Express do after it became successful? It tried to be all things to all people. It invested in new equipment, like 747s. It started to fly the heavily traveled routes to places like Chicago and Denver, not to mention Europe. It bought Frontier Airlines. It added frills, like first-class sections.

People Express promptly lost altitude and only escaped bankruptcy court by selling itself to Texas Air, which did it for them.

White Castle, on the other hand, has never changed its position. A White Castle today not only looks the same as a White Castle did 60 years ago, it also sells the same "frozen sliders" at unbelievably low prices. Would you believe the average White Castle does more than $1 million a year in revenues? (That's more than Burger King and not too far behind McDonald's.)

Good things come to those who sacrifice.

14
The Law of Attributes

For every attribute, there is an opposite, effective attribute.

In chapter 6 (The Law of Exclusivity) we made the point that you can't own the same word or position that your competitor owns. You must find your own word to own. You must seek out another attribute.

Too often a company attempts to emulate the leader. "They must know what works," goes the rationale, "so let's do something similar." Not good thinking.

It's much better to search for an opposite attribute that will allow you to play off against the leader. The key word here is *opposite—similar* won't do.

Coca-Cola was the original and thus the choice of older people. Pepsi successfully positioned itself as the choice of the younger generation.

Since Crest owned *cavities,* other toothpastes avoided cavities and jumped on other attributes like taste, whitening, breath protection, and, more recently, baking soda.

Marketing is a battle of ideas. So if you are to succeed, you must have an idea or attribute of your own to focus your efforts around. Without one, you had better have a low price. A very low price.

Some say all attributes are not created equal. Some attributes are more important to customers than others. You must try and own the most important attribute.

Cavity prevention is the most important attribute in toothpaste. It's the one to own. But the law of exclusivity points to the simple truth that once an attribute is successfully taken by your competition, it's gone. You must move on to a lesser attribute and live with a smaller share of the category. Your job is to seize a different attribute, dramatize the value of your attribute, and thus increase your share.

For many years IBM dominated the world of computers with its attributes of "big" and "powerful." Companies that tried to move in on those attributes had little success. RCA, GE, UNIVAC, Burroughs, Honeywell, NCR, and Control Data lost a lot of money on mainframe computers. Then an upstart from Boston went for the attribute of "small" and the minicomputer was born. They probably laughed in Armonk because they knew corporate America wanted "big and powerful." Today "small" has grown to such proportions that IBM's vast mainframe empire is in serious trouble.

A company that never laughs at new attributes that are exactly the opposite of their current products is Gillette, the world's No. 1 razor blade maker. Its dominance revolves around its high-technology razors and cartridge systems. When an upstart from France brought an opposite attribute to the category in the form of a "disposable" razor, Gillette could have laughed and wheeled out its research on how America wants hefty, expensive, high-technology razors. But it didn't.

Instead, Gillette jumped in with a disposable razor of its own, called Good News. By spending heavily, Gillette was able to win the battle of the disposables.

Today the Gillette Good News razor dominates the disposable category, which has grown to dominate the razor blade business. Moral: You can't predict the size of a new attribute's share, so never laugh.

Burger King was unsuccessful when it tried to take the attribute "fast" from McDonald's. What should Burger King have done? Use the opposite attribute? The exact opposite attribute, "slow," won't do for a fast-food place (although there is an element of slowness in Burger King's "broiling" concept).

A single trip to any McDonald's should be enough to find another attribute that McDonald's owns: "kids." This is indeed the place to which kids drag their parents, and McDonald's has the swing sets to prove it. This sets up an opportunity vividly demonstrated by the Coke and Pepsi battle. If McDonald's owns kids, then Burger King has the opportunity to position itself for the older crowd, which includes any kid who doesn't want to be perceived as a kid. That generally works out to be everyone over the age of 10 (not a bad market).

To make the concept work, Burger King would have to invoke the law of sacrifice and give all the little kids to McDonald's. While this might mean getting rid of a few swing sets, it also allows Burger King to hang "kiddieland" on McDonald's (chapter 9: The Law of the Opposite).

To drive the concept into prospects' minds, Burger King would need a term. It could be *grow up.* Grow up to the flame-broiled taste of Burger King.

The new concept for Burger King would strike fear and terror in the boardroom at McDonald's, always a good sign of an effective program.

15
The Law of Candor

When you admit a negative, the prospect will give you a positive.

"THE TASTE YOU HATE TWICE A DAY"

It goes against corporate and human nature to admit a problem. For years, the power of positive thinking has been drummed into us. "Think positive" has been the subject of endless books and articles.

So it may come as a surprise to you that one of the most effective ways to get into a prospect's mind is to first admit a negative and then twist it into a positive.

"Avis is only No. 2 in rent-a-cars."

"With a name like Smucker's, it has to be good."

"The 1970 VW will stay ugly longer."

"Joy. The most expensive perfume in the world."

What's going on here? Why does a dose of honesty work so well in the marketing process?

First and foremost, candor is very disarming. Every negative statement you make about yourself is instantly accepted as truth. Positive statements, on the other hand, are looked at as dubious at best. Especially in an advertisement.

You have to prove a positive statement to the prospect's satisfaction. No proof is needed for a negative statement.

"The 1970 VW will stay ugly longer." A car that ugly must be reliable, thinks the prospect.

"Joy. The most expensive perfume in the world." If people are willing to pay $375 an ounce, it must be a sensational perfume.

"With a name like Smucker's, it has to be good." Most companies, especially family companies, would never make fun of their own name. Yet the Smucker family did, which is one reason why Smucker's is the

No. 1 brand of jams and jellies. If your name is bad, you have two choices: change the name or make fun of it. The one thing you can't do is to ignore a bad name. Which is one reason why you won't find beer brands like Gablinger's, Grolsch, and Gresedieck in your supermarket today.

"Avis is only No. 2 in rent-a-cars." So why go with them? They must try harder. Everybody knew that Avis was second in rent-a-cars.

So why go with the obvious? Marketing is often a search for the obvious. Since you can't change a mind once it's made up, your marketing efforts have to be devoted to using ideas and concepts already installed in the brain. You have to use your marketing programs to "rub it in." No program did this as brilliantly as the Avis No. 2 program.

Positive thinking has been highly overrated. The explosive growth of communications in our society has made people defensive and cautious about companies trying to sell them anything. Admitting a problem is something that very few companies do.

When a company starts a message by admitting a problem, people tend to, almost instinctively, open their minds. Think about the times that someone came to you with a problem and how quickly you got involved and wanted to help. Now think about people starting off a conversation about some wonderful things they are doing. You probably were a lot less interested.

Now with that mind open, you're in a position to drive in the positive, which is your selling idea. Some years ago, Scope entered the mouthwash market with a "good-tasting" mouthwash, thus exploiting Listerine's truly terrible taste.

What should Listerine do? It certainly couldn't tell people that Listerine's taste "wasn't all that bad." That would raise a red flag that would reinforce a negative perception. Things could get worse. Instead, Listerine brilliantly invoked the law of candor: "The taste you hate twice a day."

Not only did the company admit the product tasted bad, it admitted that people actually hated it. (Now that's honesty.) This set up the selling idea that Listerine "kills a lot of germs."

The prospect figured that anything that tastes like disinfectant must indeed be a germ killer. A crisis passed with the help of a heavy dose of candor.

As another example, General Foods admitted that Grape-Nuts cereal was a "learned pleasure" and advised consumers to "try it for a week." Sales went up 23 percent.

One final note: The law of candor must be used carefully and with great skill. First, your "negative" must be widely perceived as a negative. It has to trigger an instant agreement with your prospect's mind. If the negative doesn't register quickly, your prospect will be confused and will wonder, "What's this all about?"

Next, you have to shift quickly to the positive. The purpose of candor isn't to apologize. The purpose of candor is to set up a benefit that will convince your prospect.

This law only proves the old maxim: Honesty is the best policy.

16
The Law of Singularity

In each situation, only one move will produce substantial results.

Many marketing people see success as the sum total of a lot of small efforts beautifully executed.

They think they can pick and choose from a number of different strategies and still be successful as long as they put enough effort into the program. If they work for the leader in the category, they fritter away their resources on a number of different programs. They seem to think that the best way to grow is the puppy approach—get into everything.

If they're not with the leader, they often end up trying to do the same as the leader, but a little better. It's like Saddam Hussein saying that all we have to do is fight a little harder and everything will work out. Trying harder is not the secret of marketing success.

Whether you try hard or try easy, the differences are marginal. Furthermore, the bigger the company, the more the law of averages wipes out any real advantage of a trying-harder approach.

History teaches that the only thing that works in marketing is the single, bold stroke. Furthermore, in any given situation there is only one move that will produce substantial results.

Successful generals study the battleground and look for that one bold stroke that is least expected by the enemy. Finding one is difficult. Finding more than one is usually impossible.

Military strategist and author B.H. Liddell Hart calls this bold stroke "the line of least expectation." The Allied invasion came at Normandy, a place whose tide and rocky shore the Germans felt would be an unlikely choice for a landing of any scale.

So it is in marketing. Most often there is only one place where a competitor is vulnerable. And that place should be the focus of the entire invading force.

The automobile industry is an interesting case in point. For years, the leader's main strength was in the middle of the line. With brands like Chevrolet, Pontiac, Oldsmobile, Buick, and Cadillac, General Motors easily beat back frontal assaults by Ford, Chrysler, and American Motors. (The Edsel fiasco is a typical example.) GM's dominance became legendary.

What works in marketing is the same as what works in the military: the unexpected.

Hannibal came over the Alps, a route deemed impossible to scale. Hitler came around the Maginot Line and sent his panzer divisions through the Ardennes, terrain the French generals thought impossible to traverse with tanks. (As a matter of fact, he did it twice—once in the Battle of France and again in the Battle of the Bulge.)

In recent years there have been only two strong moves made against GM. Both were flanking moves around the GM Maginot Line. The Japanese came at the low end with small cars like Toyota, Datsun, and Honda. The Germans came at the high end with superpremium cars like Mercedes and BMW.

With the success of Japanese and German flanking attacks, General Motors was under pressure to commit resources in an attempt to shore up the bottom and the top of its lines. (Cadillacs were too cheap to block the high-priced German imports.)

In an effort to save money and maintain profits,

GM made the fateful decision to build many of its midrange cars using the same body style. Suddenly, no one could tell a Chevrolet from a Pontiac or an Oldsmobile or a Buick. They all looked alike.

Its look-alike cars weakened General Motors in the middle and opened up a move for Ford as it broke through with the European-styled Taurus and Sable. And then the Japanese jumped in with Acura, Lexus, and Infiniti. Now General Motors is weak across the board.

Look at Coke. At present, Coca-Cola is fighting a two-front battle with Classic and New Coke. While Coca-Cola Classic has regained a lot of its original strength, New Coke (an Edsel from Atlanta) is barely hanging on.

We've seen endless slogans for Coca-Cola: "We have a taste for you." "The real choice." "Catch the Wave." "Red, white, and you." "You can't beat the feeling." And now, "You can't beat the real thing." Nothing has moved the needle very much.

The folks at Coca-Cola keep trying. They've even hired a Hollywood talent agency to contribute creative ideas.

Any day now, the new shooters will parade into an Atlanta conference room and paper the wall with a new set of slogans. Top Coke management will then sit around and discuss the latest batch of creative moves. While it's theoretically possible to stumble across the right idea if you haphazardly generate all the ideas you can possibly think of, it's not an efficient way to work.

Coke needs to make progress beyond just buying business. As we see it, Coke has only one two-part move to make—one part is a step backward, the other is a step forward.

First of all, Coke has to bite the bullet and drop New Coke. Not because it's a loser or an embarrassment, but because the existence of New Coke blocks the company from effectively using the only weapon it has.

With New Coke safely tucked away in the archives, Coke would be able to invoke the law of focus and bring back the concept of the "Real Thing" and use it against Pepsi.

To pull the trigger, Coke could go on television and say to the Pepsi Generation, "All right kids, we're not going to push you. When you're ready for the Real Thing, we've got it for you." That would be the beginning of the end of the Pepsi Generation (if Pepsi-Cola hadn't already killed it off all by itself).

Not only is this idea simple and powerful, but it's really the only move available to Coke. It exploits the only words that Coke owns in the minds of its prospects: *The Real Thing.*

To find that singular idea or concept, marketing managers have to know what's happening in the marketplace. They have to be down at the front in the mud of the battle. They have to know what's working and what isn't. They have to be involved.

Because of the high cost of mistakes, management can't afford to delegate important marketing decisions. That's what happened at General Motors.

When the financial people took over, the marketing programs collapsed. Their interest was in the numbers, not the brands. The irony is that the numbers went south, along with the brands.

It's hard to find that single move if you're hanging around headquarters and not involved in the process.

17
The Law of Unpredictability

Unless you write your competitors' plans, you can't predict the future.

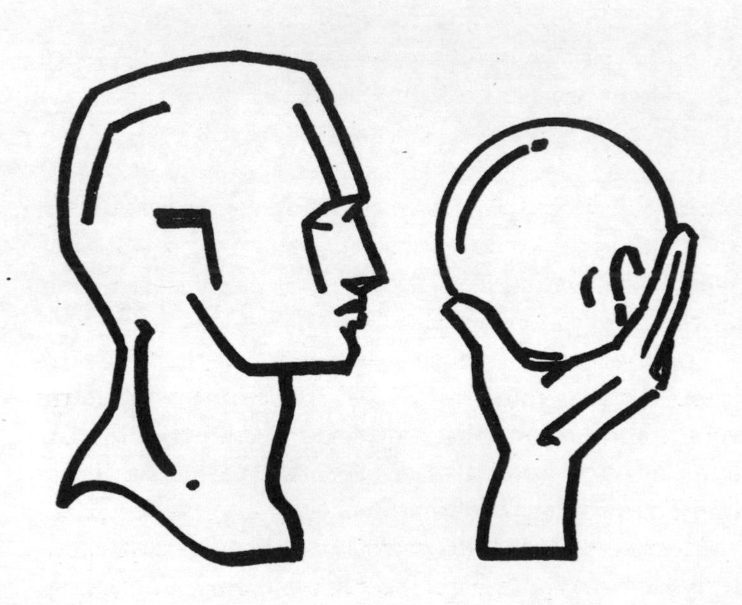

Implicit in most marketing plans is an assumption about the future. Yet marketing plans based on what will happen in the future are usually wrong.

With hundreds of computers and an army of meteorologists, no one can predict the weather three days in advance, so how do you expect to predict your market three years in advance?

IBM developed a massive marketing plan to hook up all PCs to its mainframes. The company called it OfficeVision. Yet the plan is dead in the water thanks to developments at Sun Microsystems, Microsoft, and other companies. You might say that OfficeVision foresaw everything but the competition.

Failure to forecast competitive reaction is a major reason for marketing failures. When Pickett was asked which Confederate leader was responsible for the defeat at Gettysburg, he replied, "I've always thought the Yankees had something to do with it."

Yet there are those who would say that America's big problem is the lack of the long view, that American management is too short term in its thinking. Won't eliminating long-term plans make things even worse?

On the surface those concerns are real. But it's important to understand what is meant by long term versus short term. Most of corporate America's problems are not related to short-term marketing thinking. The problem is short-term financial thinking.

Most companies live from quarterly report to quarterly report. That's a recipe for problems. Companies that live by the numbers, die by the numbers. Harold Geneen of ITT fame is one man in recent times who best exemplifies this approach. He would wheel and deal and beat up his managers for ever-increasing earnings.

Geneen's efforts resulted in a house of cards that eventually fell apart. Today ITT is a shell of what it once was. Good accounting, bad marketing.

General Motors was doing fine until the financial folks took over and put the focus on the numbers instead of the brands. They allowed Alfred P. Sloan's plan of differentiated brands to fall apart. Every division head, in order to make their short-term numbers, started to chase the middle of the market.

Good short-term planning is coming up with that angle or word that differentiates your product or company. Then you set up a coherent long-term marketing direction that builds a program to maximize that idea or angle. It's not a long-term plan, it's a long-term direction.

Tom Monaghan's short-term angle at Domino's Pizza was to come up with that "home delivery" idea and build a system that delivered pizzas quickly and efficiently. His long-term direction was to build the first nationwide home delivery chain as rapidly as possible.

Monaghan couldn't own the words *home delivery* until he had enough franchisees to afford national advertising. He accomplished both objectives, and today Domino's is a $2.65 billion company with a 40 percent share of the home delivery business. Monaghan did it all without a complex, 10-year plan.

So what can you do? How can you best cope with unpredictability? While you can't predict the future, you can get a handle on trends, which is a way to take advantage of change. One example of a trend is America's growing orientation toward good health. This trend has opened the door for a number of new products, especially healthier foods. The recent runaway success of Healthy Choice frozen entrées is a clear example of a product that took advantage of this long-term trend.

ConAgra introduced Healthy Choice in March 1989. Years earlier, however, there were plenty of low-sodium, low-fat, light brands on the market. But these healthy ideas were buried under line extension names. ConAgra was the first to use a simple name and concept to take advantage of a trend that has been going on for years.

Unfortunately, ConAgra is well on its way to confusing things with a wide array of Healthy Choice line extensions that go way beyond entrées. It is violating the law of sacrifice.

The danger in working with trends is extrapolation. Many companies jump to conclusions about how far a trend will go. If you believed the prognosticators of a few years ago, everyone today is eating broiled fish or mesquite-barbecued chicken. (Hamburger sales are doing just fine, thank you.)

Equally as bad as extrapolating a trend is the common practice of assuming the future will be a replay of the present. When you assume that nothing will change, you are predicting the future just as surely as when you assume that something will change. Remember Peter's Law: The unexpected always happens.

While tracking trends can be a useful tool in dealing with the unpredictable future, market research can be more of a problem than a help. Research does best at measuring the past. New ideas and concepts are almost impossible to measure. No one has a frame of reference. People don't know what they will do until they face an actual decision.

The classic example is the research conducted before Xerox introduced the plain-paper copier. What came back was the conclusion that no one would pay five cents for a plain-paper copy when they could get a Thermofax copy for a cent and a half.

Xerox ignored the research, and the rest is history.

One way to cope with an unpredictable world is to build an enormous amount of flexibility into your organization. As change comes sweeping through your category, you have to be willing to change and change quickly if you are to survive in the long term.

Yesterday, General Motors was slow to react to the small-car trend. It has cost the company dearly.

Today, IBM is slow to acknowledge the trend away from mainframes. It could cost the company dearly.

At present, the workstation is a real threat to both mainframes and minicomputers. It offers enormous power at very low cost. If IBM is going to protect its computer leadership, the company must become a serious player in a category dominated by Sun Microsystems and Hewlett-Packard.

A natural move would be to introduce a new generic. IBM's best opportunity might be to name its new line of high-powered workstations "PMs," just as it did with its very successful "PCs." "PM" could stand for "personal mainframe." These two generic words dramatically capture the speed and power of these new desktop machines. They are also words that IBM owns in the mind. The combination would be very powerful.

The only problem with a concept like this probably lies inside IBM itself. The term *personal mainframe* would strike terror in IBM's mainframe division as well as in its personal computer division. We suggest that the phones would ring and the case would quickly be made that a "personal mainframe" would undermine these two important sources of income.

It's probably true that a personal mainframe product would undermine IBM's two other main sources of revenue, but a company must be flexible enough to attack itself with a new idea. Change isn't easy, but it's the only way to cope with an unpredictable future.

One final note that's worth mentioning: There's a difference between "predicting" the future and "taking a chance" on the future. Orville Redenbacher's Gourmet Popping Corn took a chance that people would pay twice as much for a high-end popcorn. Not a bad risk in today's affluent society.

No one can predict the future with any degree of certainty. Nor should marketing plans try to.

18
The Law of Success

Success often leads to arrogance, and arrogance to failure.

Ego is the enemy of successful marketing.

Objectivity is what's needed.

When people become successful, they tend to become less objective. They often substitute their own judgment for what the market wants.

Donald Trump and Robert Maxwell are two examples of people blinded by early success and untainted by humility. And when you're blind, it is indeed hard to focus.

Mr. Trump's strategy was to put his name on everything, committing the cardinal sin of line extension. (Denial seems to go hand in hand with a big ego. When we first met The Donald, his opening remarks were about how people accuse him of having a big ego. He went on to state that it was totally untrue, he did not have a big ego. All the while, it was hard to avoid noticing a three-foot-high brass "T" sitting on the floor next to his desk. So much for the sermon.)

Success is often the fatal element behind the rash of line extensions. When a brand is successful, the company assumes the name is the primary reason for the brand's success. So they promptly look for other products to plaster the name on.

Actually it's the opposite. The name didn't make the brand famous (although a bad name might keep the brand from becoming famous). The brand got famous because you made the right marketing moves. In other words, the steps you took were in tune with the fundamental laws of marketing.

You got into the mind first. You narrowed the

focus. You preempted a powerful attribute.

Your success puffs up your ego to such an extent that you put the famous name on other products. Result: early success and long-term failure as illustrated by the failure of Donald Trump.

The more you identify with your brand or corporate name, the more likely you are to fall into the line extension trap. "It can't be the name," you might be thinking when things go wrong. "We have a great name." Pride goeth before destruction and a haughty spirit before a fall. Proverbs 16:18.

Tom Monaghan of Domino's Pizza is one of the few executives who have recognized how ego can lead you astray. "You start thinking you can do anything. I was that way back in the early days. I got into frozen pizzas for a while and that was a disaster. If I hadn't messed around with those frozen pizzas for the better part of a year, trying to sell them in bars and restaurants, Domino's probably would have a lot more stores by now."

Actually, ego is helpful. It can be an effective driving force in building a business. What hurts is injecting your ego in the marketing process. Brilliant marketers have the ability to think like a prospect thinks. They put themselves in the shoes of their customers. They don't impose their own view of the world on the situation. (Keep in mind that the world is all perception anyway, and the only thing that counts in marketing is the customer's perception.)

As their successes mounted, companies like General Motors, Sears, Roebuck, and IBM became arrogant. They felt they could do anything they wanted to in the marketplace. Success leads to failure.

Consider Digital Equipment Corporation, the company that brought us the minicomputer. Starting from scratch, DEC became an enormously successful $14 billion company.

DEC's founder is Kenneth Olsen. His success made Ken such a believer in his own view of the computer world that he pooh-poohed the personal computer, then open systems, and, finally, reduced instruction set computing (RISC). In other words, Ken Olsen ignored three of the biggest developments in the computer category. (A trend is like the tide—you don't fight it.) Today Ken Olsen is out.

The bigger the company, the more likely it is that the chief executive has lost touch with the front lines. This might be the single most important factor limiting the growth of a corporation. All other factors favor size. Marketing is war, and the first principle of warfare is the principle of force. The larger army, the larger company, has the advantage.

But the larger company gives up some of that advantage if it cannot keep itself focused on the marketing battle that takes place in the mind of the customer.

The shootout at General Motors between Roger Smith and Ross Perot illustrates the point. When he was on the GM board, Ross Perot spent his weekends visiting dealers and buying cars. He was critical of Roger Smith for not doing the same.

"We've got to nuke the GM system," Perot said. He

advocated atom-bombing the heated garages, chauffeur-driven limousines, executive dining rooms. (Chauffeur-driven limousines for a company trying to sell cars?)

If you're a busy CEO, how do you gather objective information on what is really happening? How do you get around the propensity of middle management to tell you what they think you want to hear?

How do you get the bad news as well as the good?

One possibility is to go "in disguise" or unannounced. This is especially useful at the distributor or retailer level. In many ways this is analogous to the king who dresses up as a commoner and mingles with his subjects. Reason: to get honest opinions of what's happening.

Like kings, chief executives rarely get honest opinions from their ministers. There's too much intrigue going on at the court.

Another aspect of the problem is the allocation of time. Quite often the CEO's time is taken up with too many United Way meetings, too many industry activities, too many outside board meetings, too many testimonial dinners.

According to one survey, the average CEO spends 18 hours a week on "outside activities." The next time-waster is internal meetings. The average CEO spends 17 hours a week attending corporate meetings and 6 hours a week preparing for those meetings. Since the typical top executive works 61 hours a week, that leaves only 20 hours for everything else, including managing the operation and going down to the front. No wonder chief executives delegate the marketing function. That's a mistake.

Marketing is too important to be turned over to an underling. If you delegate anything, you should delegate the chairmanship of the next fund-raising drive. (The vice president of the United States, not the president, attends the state funerals.) The next thing to cut back on are the meetings. Instead of talking things over, walk out and see for yourself. As Gorbachev told Reagan, "It is better to see once than to hear a hundred times."

Small companies are mentally closer to the front than big companies. That might be one reason they grew more rapidly in the last decade. They haven't been tainted by the law of success.

19
The Law of Failure

Failure is to be expected and accepted.

Too many companies try to fix things rather than drop things. "Let's reorganize to save the situation" is their way of life.

Admitting a mistake and not doing anything about it is bad for your career. A better strategy is to recognize failure early and cut your losses. American Motors should have abandoned passenger cars and focused on Jeep. IBM should have dropped copiers and Xerox should have dropped computers years before they finally recognized their mistakes.

The Japanese seem to be able to admit a mistake early and then make the necessary changes. Their consensus management style tends to eliminate the ego. Since a large number of people have a small piece of a big decision, there is no stigma that can be considered career damaging. In other words, it's a lot easer to live with "We were all wrong" than the devastating "I was wrong."

This egoless approach is a major factor in making the Japanese such relentless marketers. It's not that they don't make mistakes, but when they do, they admit them, fix them, and just keep coming.

The hugely successful Wal-Mart has another approach that enables the company to deal with failure. It's called Sam Walton's "ready, fire, aim" approach. It's an outgrowth of his penchant for constant tinkering.

Walton was well aware that nobody hits the target every time. But at Wal-Mart, people aren't punished if their experiments fail. As Wal-Mart's chief executive said in a *Business Week* article, "If you learn something and you're trying something, then you probably get credit for it. But woe to the person who makes the same mistake twice."

Wal-Mart is different from many large corporations because, so far, it appears to be free of an insidious disease called the "personal agenda" that can creep into any corporation. Marketing decisions are often made first with the decision maker's career in mind and second with the impact on the competition or the enemy in mind. There is a built-in conflict between the personal and the corporate agenda.

This leads to a failure to take risks. (It's hard to be first in a new category without sticking your neck out.) When the senior executive has a high salary and a short time to retirement, a bold move is highly unlikely.

Even junior executives often make "safe" decisions so as to not disrupt their progress up the corporate ladder. Nobody has ever been fired for a bold move they didn't make.

In some American companies nothing gets done unless it benefits the personal agenda of someone in top management. This severely limits the potential marketing moves a company can make. An idea gets rejected not because it isn't fundamentally sound but because no one in top management will personally benefit from its success.

One way to defuse the personal agenda factor is to bring it out in the open. 3M uses the "champion" system to publicly identify the person who will benefit from the success of a new product or venture. The successful introduction of 3M's Post-it Notes illustrates how the concept works. Art Fry is the 3M scientist who championed the Post-it Notes product, which took almost a dozen years to bring to market.

While the 3M system works, in theory the ideal environment would allow managers to judge a concept on its merits, not on whom the concept would benefit.

If a company is going to operate in an ideal way, it will take teamwork, esprit de corps, and a self-sacrificing leader. One immediately thinks of Patton and his Third Army and its dash across France. No army in history took as much territory and as many prisoners in as short a period of time.

Patton's reward? Eisenhower fired him.

20
The Law of Hype

The situation is often the opposite of the way it appears in the press.

When IBM was successful, the company said very little. Now it throws a lot of press conferences.

When things are going well, a company doesn't need the hype. When you need the hype, it usually means you're in trouble.

Young and inexperienced reporters and editors tend to be more impressed by what they read in other publications than by what they gather themselves. Once the hype starts, it often continues on and on.

No soft drink has received more hype than New Coke. By one estimate, New Coke received more than $1 billion worth of free publicity. Add to that the hundreds of millions of dollars spent to launch the brand, and New Coke should have been the world's most successful product. It didn't happen.

Less than 60 days after the launch, Coca-Cola was forced to come back with the original formula, now called Coca-Cola Classic. Today Classic outsells New about 15 to 1.

No newspaper has received more hype than *USA Today*. At its launch in 1982 were the president of the United States, the speaker of the House of Representatives, and the majority leader of the U.S. Senate. The residue of this initial hype is still so great that most people cannot believe *USA Today* is a loser.

No computer has received more hype than the NeXt computer. Demand for press conference credentials was so great that Steve Jobs had to print tickets in advance, even though the auditorium could hold several thousand people. All the seats were filled.

Steve Jobs makes television news as well as the cover of many major publications. IBM, Ross Perot, and Canon have invested $130 million.

Will NeXt be a winner? Of course not. Where is the opening? NeXt is the first in a new category of what?

History is filled with marketing failures that were successful in the press. The Tucker 48, the U.S. Football League, Videotext, the automated factory, the personal helicopter, the manufactured home, the picturephone, polyester suits. The essence of the hype was not just that the new product was going to be successful. The essence of the hype was that existing products would now be obsolete.

Polyester was going to make wool obsolete. Videotext was going to make newspapers obsolete. The personal helicopter was going to make the roads and highways obsolete. The Tucker 48 with its "cyclop's eye" headlight would revolutionize the way Detroit makes automobiles. (Only 51 were ever built.)

In the heavily touted "office of the future," everything was going to be integrated into one ball of computer wax. The last time we looked, there were separate typewriters (now called personal computers), separate laser printers, separate fax machines, separate copy machines, separate postal meters. The office of the future is aptly named—a concept that will remain forever in the future.

These predictions violate the law of unpredictability. No one can predict the future, not even a sophisticated reporter for the *Wall Street Journal*. The only revolutions you can predict are the ones that have already started.

Did anyone predict the overthrow of communism and the Soviet Union? Not really. It was only after the process had started that the press jumped on the "crumbling communist empire" story.

Contrast the first Tucker with the first Toyopet that hit the shores of California. Did the *Los Angeles Times* do a story on how Japanese imports were going to shake up the auto industry? Not at all. The only stories that made the news were about the little cars from Japan that fell apart because they weren't up to the rigors of American roads. (Toyopet, of course, went on to become a big winner after changing the cars and changing the car's name to Toyota.)

When MCI got started by launching a microwave service between Chicago and St. Louis, did the press say, "Watch out, AT&T, here comes the competition?" No, they pretty much ignored little MCI. When Sun Microsystems shipped its first workstation, did the press note the significance of the event, that someday workstations would rattle the cages at IBM and DEC? No, the press ignored Sun.

Forget the front page. If you're looking for clues to the future, look in the back of the paper for those innocuous little stories.

Neither the personal computer nor the facsimile machine took off like a rocket. The personal computer was introduced in 1974. It took six years for IBM to strike back with the PC. Even the PC didn't boom until a year and a half later, when *Lotus 1-2-3* hit the market.

Capturing the imagination of the public is not the same as revolutionizing a market. Take the picture-phone, now called the videophone. Ever since its introduction at the 1964 New York World's Fair, the picturephone has been in the news, usually on the front page. The latest example is a front-page story in the *Wall Street Journal,* "The Videophone Era May Finally Be Near, Bringing Big Changes."

This is the third try for AT&T. In the seventies, it failed with the picturephone at $100 a month. In the eighties, it failed with a picturephone meeting service at $2,300 an hour. In the nineties, AT&T is hustling $1,500 videophones.

It's easy to see why the videophone hasn't made much progress. Who wants to get dressed up to make a phone call?

What isn't so easy to see is why the videophone gets so much hype. There's a clue in the subhead of the *Journal* article, "An Alternative To Travel." Look out American Airlines, United, and Delta, your days are numbered. The hype really isn't about the video-phone at all. It's about the coming revolution in the travel industry.

Over the years, the greatest hype has been for those developments that promise to single-handedly change an entire industry, preferably one that's vital to the American economy. Remember the helicopter hype after World War II? Every garage would house a heli-copter, making roads, bridges, and the entire automobile industry obsolete overnight. Did Donald Trump get a helicopter? Did you get yours? (Donald actually did get his, but he had to give it back to the bank.)

Then there was the manufactured-home hype. It was reported that the single most expensive product a family ever buys could be made on the assembly line, revolutionizing the construction industry.

From time to time, no-frills food makes the headlines. It is reported that this development will revolutionize the packaged-goods industry. Brands are out. People will read the labels and buy products on their merits rather than on the size of the brand's advertising budget. It's all hype.

The latest overhyped development is that of the pen computer, which will revolutionize the personal computer field and make computers accessible to everyone whether they can type or not. It's all hype.

Not that there isn't a grain of truth in every overhyped story. Anyone with $580,000 plus tax can buy a little five-seat Bell helicopter. The pen computer might be attractive to a narrow segment of the market, especially the traveling-salesperson crowd. The videophone could revolutionize the phone-sex industry, and there's a substantial market for mobile homes and recreational vehicles, all manufactured on assembly lines.

But, for the most part, hype is hype. Real revolutions don't arrive at high noon with marching bands and coverage on the 6:00 P.M. news. Real revolutions arrive unannounced in the middle of the night and kind of sneak up on you.

21
The Law of Acceleration

Successful programs are not built on fads, they're built on trends.

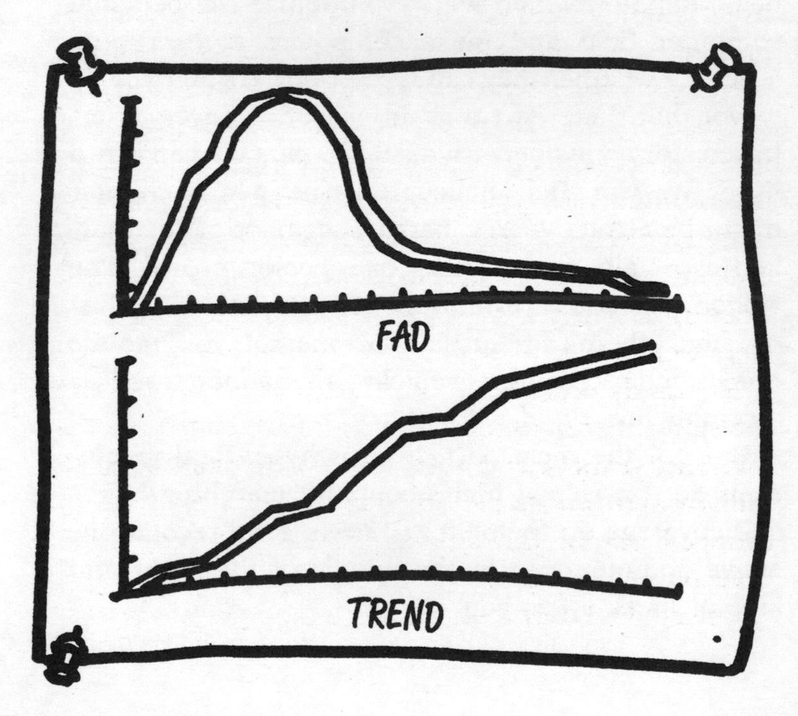

A fad is a wave in the ocean, and a trend is the tide. A fad gets a lot of hype, and a trend gets very little.

Like a wave, a fad is very visible, but it goes up and down in a big hurry. Like the tide, a trend is almost invisible, but it's very powerful over the long term.

A fad is a short-term phenomenon that might be profitable, but a fad doesn't last long enough to do a company much good. Furthermore, a company often tends to gear up as if a fad were a trend. As a result, the company is often stuck with a lot of staff, expensive manufacturing facilities, and distribution networks.

(A fashion, on the other hand, is a fad that repeats itself. Examples: short skirts for women and double-breasted suits for men. Halley's Comet is a fashion because it comes back every 75 years or so.)

When the fad disappears, a company often goes into a deep financial shock. What happened to Atari is typical in this respect. And look how Coleco Industries handled the Cabbage Patch Kids. Those homely dolls hit the market in 1983 and started to take off. Coleco's strategy was to milk the kids for all they were worth.

Hundreds of Cabbage Patch novelties flooded the toy stores. Pens, pencils, crayon boxes, games, clothing. Two years later, Coleco racked up sales of $776 million and profits of $83 million. Then the bottom dropped out of the Cabbage Patch Kids. By 1988 Coleco went into Chapter 11.

Coleco died, but the kids live on. Acquired by Hasbro in 1989, the Cabbage Patch Kids are now being handled conservatively. Today they're doing quite well.

Here's the paradox. If you were faced with a rapidly rising business, with all the characteristics of a fad, the best thing you could do would be to dampen the fad. By dampening the fad, you stretch the fad out and it becomes more like a trend.

You see this in the toy business. Some owners of hot toys want to put their hot toy name on everything. The result is that it becomes an enormous fad that is bound to collapse. When everybody has a Ninja turtle, nobody wants one anymore.

The Ninja turtle is a good example of a fad that collapses in a hurry because the owner of the concept got greedy. The owner fans the fad rather than dampening it.

On the other hand, the Barbie doll is a trend. When Barbie was invented years ago, the doll was never heavily merchandised into other areas. As a result, the Barbie doll has become a long-term trend in the toy business.

The most successful entertainers are the ones who control their appearances. They don't overextend themselves. They're not all over the place. They don't wear out their welcome.

Elvis Presley's manager, Colonel Parker, made a deliberate attempt to restrict the number of appearances and records the King made. As a result, every time Elvis appeared, it was an event of enormous impact. (Elvis himself contributed to this strategy by overdosing early and severely dampening his future appearances. Likewise Marilyn Monroe and James Dean.)

Forget fads. And when they appear, try to dampen them. One way to maintain a long-term demand for your product is to never totally satisfy the demand.

But the best, most profitable thing to ride in marketing is a long-term trend.

22
The Law of Resources

Without adequate funding an idea won't get off the ground.

If you have a good idea and you've picked up this book with the thought in mind that all you need is a little marketing help, this chapter will throw cold water on that thought.

Even the best idea in the world won't go very far without the money to get it off the ground. Inventors, entrepreneurs, and assorted idea generators seem to think that all their good ideas need is professional marketing help.

Nothing could be further from the truth. Marketing is a game fought in the mind of the prospect. You need money to get into a mind. And you need money to stay in the mind once you get there.

You'll get further with a mediocre idea and a million dollars than with a great idea alone.

Some entrepreneurs see advertising as the solution to the problem of getting into prospects' minds. Advertising is expensive. It cost $9,000 a minute to fight World War II. It cost $22,000 a minute to fight the Vietnam War. A one-minute commercial on the NFL Super Bowl will cost you $1.5 million.

Steve Jobs and Steve Wozniak had a great idea. But it was Mike Markkula's $91,000 that put Apple Computer on the map. (For his money, Markkula got one-third of Apple. He should have held out for half.)

Ideas without money are worthless. Well... not quite. But you have to use your idea to find the money, not the marketing help. The marketing can come later.

Some entrepreneurs see publicity as a cheap way

of getting into prospects' minds. "Free advertising" is how they see it. Publicity isn't free. Rule of thumb: 5-10-20. A small public relations agency will want $5,000 a month to promote your product; a medium-size agency, $10,000 a month; and a big-time agency, $20,000 a month.

Some entrepreneurs see venture capitalists as the solution to their money problems. But only a tiny percentage succeed in finding the funding they need this way.

Some entrepreneurs see corporate America as ready, willing, and financially able to get their off-spring off the ground. Good luck, you'll need it. Very few outside ideas are ever accepted by large companies. Your only real hope is finding a smaller company and persuading it of the merits of your idea.

Remember: An idea without money is worthless. Be prepared to give away a lot for the funding.

In marketing, the rich often get richer because they have the resources to drive their ideas into the mind. Their problem is separating the good ideas from the bad ones, and avoiding spending money on too many products and too many programs (chapter 5: The Law of Focus).

Competition is fierce. The giant corporations put a lot of money behind their brands. Procter & Gamble and Philip Morris each spend more than $2 billion a year on advertising. General Motors spends $1.5 billion a year.

Life can be unfair for the smaller marketer facing larger competitors. Consider A&M Pet Products, a small company in Houston, Texas. A&M invented "clumping" cat litter, one of the most important breakthroughs in the category. The concept is simple. When cats use the litter box, this new type of litter clumps the waste into balls, which are easily scooped out and disposed of. There is no need to replace the entire box.

The brand, called Scoop Away, took off wherever it was introduced. This quickly got the attention of Golden Cat Corporation, which has the No. 1 cat litter brand, Tidy Cat.

Recognizing a threatening idea when they see one, Golden Cat introduced their own version of clumping cat litter, called Tidy Scoop. Not only did they jump on A&M's idea, they also borrowed the *Scoop* part of their brand name. (How unfair can you be?)

The winner of this cat fight will probably be determined by money. Who has the most money to drive in the idea?

Unlike a consumer product, a technical or business product has to raise less marketing money because the prospect list is shorter and media is less expensive. But there is still a need for adequate funding for a technical product to pay for brochures, sales presentations, and trade shows as well as advertising.

Here is the bottom line. First get the idea, then go get the money to exploit it. Here are some short cuts you could take:

- You can marry the money. Georgette Mosbacher married Commerce Secretary Robert Mosbacher in 1985. Three years later, Ms. Mosbacher bought La Prairie, a Swiss cosmetics firm, for $31.5 million. Where did she get the money? From everyone. Venture capitalists, La Prairie distributors in Switzerland and Japan, plus her own and her husband's resources. In the first year under Georgette Mosbacher's control, La Prairie's sales were up 30 percent. Then she sold out at a hefty profit.

- You can divorce the money. Frances Lear arrived in New York in 1985 at the age of 61. Freshly divorced from her television producer-husband Norman ("All in the Family") Lear, she was determined to launch a magazine for women over 40. She was prepared to spend $25 million of her expected $112 million settlement on the project. By its fifth issue, *Lear's* magazine had 350,000 readers.
- You can find the money at home. Donald Trump would never have gotten anywhere without Dad's millions behind him.
- You can "share" your idea by franchising it. Tom Monaghan was able to put Domino's Pizza on the map by pursuing an aggressive program of franchising his home delivery idea.

So far we've been talking about smaller companies and their fund-raising strategies. What about a rich company? How should it approach the law of resources? The answer is simple: Spend enough. In war, the military always errs on the high side. Do you know how many rations were left after Operation Desert Storm? A lot. So it is in marketing. You can't save your way to success.

The more successful marketers front load their investment. In other words, they take no profit for two or three years as they plow all earnings back into marketing.

Money makes the marketing world go round. If you want to be successful today, you'll have to find the money you need to spin those marketing wheels.

Warning

We would be remiss if we did not warn our readers about the potential dangers of trying to apply the laws of marketing within an existing organization. Many of these laws fly in the face of corporate ego, conventional wisdom, and the Malcolm Baldrige awards.

The law of perception runs counter to the corporate culture of most companies where trying to be better is deeply ingrained. People are forever running around and "benchmarking" the leader in the category and then setting out to "beat their specs." It's what the quality movement is all about.

The law of leadership is tough for many to swallow. Most people want to believe they got to the top by being better, not by being first.

So beware! Management won't take kindly to any suggestions that will take the emphasis off their better product strategy.

The law of sacrifice could cause you problems. Offering everything for everybody is deeply ingrained in most organizations. If you have any doubts, just stroll down the aisles of any supermarket. What you will find is variation upon variation of sizes, flavors, and forms. It boggles the mind. Why this happens is painfully obvious. Nobody wants to focus.

Large companies have offices filled with young, bright marketing people. Do you expect them to just sit there and do nothing? They feel compelled to tinker and make improvements. After all, how can they make their mark on the organization?

So beware! Those young, bright marketing people will not take kindly to any efforts to curtail their tinkering.

The law of focus suggests owning a word in the prospects' minds. What word does your company own in the minds of your prospects? "I don't know," might be your response. "We make a variety of products for many different industries."

So beware! You have some pruning to do, which isn't going to be easy to sell to the powers that be.

The law of perspective will frustrate anyone looking for quick marketing victories. Companies want to see instant results.

So beware! Those accountants will give you a hard time in the short term.

The law of line extension is the most dangerous law of all to deal with. In this case, you have to be prepared to demolish what management holds to be a basic truth: Big successful brands have an equity that can be exploited to encompass different kinds of products.

Line extension makes eminent sense in the boardroom. You won't find one director in a dozen who would be willing to challenge management on this critical issue.

So beware! Management will not take kindly to any efforts to curtail their equity expansions. You may just have to wait them out. Management is mutable, but the laws of marketing are not.

Thus are you duly warned. If you violate the immutable laws, you run the risk of failure. If you apply the immutable laws, you run the risk of being bad-mouthed, ignored, or even ostracized.

Have patience. The immutable laws of marketing will help you achieve success. And success is the best revenge of all.

Index